Margaret Ogilvy

Margaret Ogilvy

J.M. Barrie

MINT EDITIONS

Margaret Ogilvy was first published in 1897.

This edition published by Mint Editions 2021.

ISBN 9781513222752 | E-ISBN 9781513222158

Published by Mint Editions®

MINT
EDITIONS

minteditionbooks.com

Publishing Director: Jennifer Newens
Design & Production: Rachel Lopez Metzger
Project Manager: Micaela Clark
Typesetting: Westchester Publishing Services

Contents

I

How My Mother Got Her Soft Face

On the day I was born we bought six hair-bottomed chairs, and in our little house it was an event, the first great victory in a woman's long campaign; how they had been laboured for, the pound-note and the thirty threepenny-bits they cost, what anxiety there was about the purchase, the show they made in possession of the west room, my father's unnatural coolness when he brought them in (but his face was white)—I so often heard the tale afterwards, and shared as boy and man in so many similar triumphs, that the coming of the chairs seems to be something I remember, as if I had jumped out of bed on that first day, and run ben to see how they looked. I am sure my mother's feet were ettling to be ben long before they could be trusted, and that the moment after she was left alone with me she was discovered barefooted in the west room, doctoring a scar (which she had been the first to detect) on one of the chairs, or sitting on them regally, or withdrawing and re-opening the door suddenly to take the six by surprise. And then, I think, a shawl was flung over her (it is strange to me to think it was not I who ran after her with the shawl), and she was escorted sternly back to bed and reminded that she had promised not to budge, to which her reply was probably that she had been gone but an instant, and the implication that therefore she had not been gone at all. Thus was one little bit of her revealed to me at once: I wonder if I took note of it. Neighbours came in to see the boy and the chairs. I wonder if she deceived me when she affected to think that there were others like us, or whether I saw through her from the first, she was so easily seen through. When she seemed to agree with them that it would be impossible to give me a college education, was I so easily taken in, or did I know already what ambitions burned behind that dear face? when they spoke of the chairs as the goal quickly reached, was I such a newcomer that her timid lips must say "They are but a beginning" before I heard the words? And when we were left together, did I laugh at the great things that were in her mind, or had she to whisper them to me first, and then did I put my arm round her and tell her that I would help? Thus it was for such a long time: it is strange to me to feel that it was not so from the beginning.

It is all guess-work for six years, and she whom I see in them is the woman who came suddenly into view when they were at an end. Her timid lips I have said, but they were not timid then, and when I knew her the timid lips had come. The soft face—they say the face was not so soft then. The shawl that was flung over her—we had not begun to hunt her with a shawl, nor to make our bodies a screen between her and the draughts, nor to creep into her room a score of times in the night to stand looking at her as she slept. We did not see her becoming little then, nor sharply turn our heads when she said wonderingly how small her arms had grown. In her happiest moments—and never was a happier woman—her mouth did not of a sudden begin to twitch, and tears to lie on the mute blue eyes in which I have read all I know and would ever care to write. For when you looked into my mother's eyes you knew, as if He had told you, why God sent her into the world—it was to open the minds of all who looked to beautiful thoughts. And that is the beginning and end of literature. Those eyes that I cannot see until I was six years old have guided me through life, and I pray God they may remain my only earthly judge to the last. They were never more my guide than when I helped to put her to earth, not whimpering because my mother had been taken away after seventy-six glorious years of life, but exulting in her even at the grave.

SHE HAD A SON WHO was far away at school. I remember very little about him, only that he was a merry-faced boy who ran like a squirrel up a tree and shook the cherries into my lap. When he was thirteen and I was half his age the terrible news came, and I have been told the face of my mother was awful in its calmness as she set off to get between Death and her boy. We trooped with her down the brae to the wooden station, and I think I was envying her the journey in the mysterious wagons; I know we played around her, proud of our right to be there, but I do not recall it, I only speak from hearsay. Her ticket was taken, she had bidden us good-bye with that fighting face which I cannot see, and then my father came out of the telegraph-office and said huskily, "He's gone!" Then we turned very quietly and went home again up the little brae. But I speak from hearsay no longer; I knew my mother forever now.

That is how she got her soft face and her pathetic ways and her large charity, and why other mothers ran to her when they had lost a child. "Dinna greet, poor Janet," she would say to them; and they would answer, "Ah, Margaret, but you're greeting yoursel." Margaret Ogilvy had been her maiden name, and after the Scotch custom she was still Margaret Ogilvy to her old friends. Margaret Ogilvy I loved to name her. Often when I was a boy, "Margaret Ogilvy, are you there?" I would call up the stair.

She was always delicate from that hour, and for many months she was very ill. I have heard that the first thing she expressed a wish to see was the christening robe, and she looked long at it and then turned her face to the wall. That was what made me as a boy think of it always as the robe in which he was christened, but I knew later that we had all been christened in it, from the oldest of the family to the youngest, between whom stood twenty years. Hundreds of other children were christened in it also, such robes being then a rare possession, and the lending of ours among my mother's glories. It was carried carefully from house to house, as if it were itself a child; my mother made much of it, smoothed it out, petted it, smiled to it before putting it into the arms of those to whom it was being lent; she was in our pew to see it borne magnificently (something inside it now) down the aisle to the pulpit-side, when a stir of expectancy went through the church and we kicked each other's feet beneath the book-board but were reverent in the face; and however the child might behave, laughing brazenly or skirling to its mother's shame, and whatever the father as he held it up might do, look doited probably and bow at the wrong time, the christening robe of long experience helped them through. And when it was brought back to her she took it in her arms as softly as if it might be asleep, and unconsciously pressed it to her breast: there was never anything in the house that spoke to her quite so eloquently as that little white robe; it was the one of her children that always remained a baby. And she had not made it herself, which was the most wonderful thing about it to me, for she seemed to have made all other things. All the clothes in the house were of her making, and you don't know her in the least if you think they were out of the fashion; she turned them and made them new again, she beat them and made them new again, and then she coaxed them into being new again just for the last time, she let them out and took them in and put on new braid, and added a piece up the back, and thus they passed from one member of the family to another until they reached the youngest, and even when we were done with them they reappeared as something else. In the fashion! I must come back to this. Never was a woman with such an eye for it. She had no fashion-plates; she did not need them. The minister's wife (a cloak), the banker's daughters (the new sleeve)—they had but to pass our window once, and the scalp, so to speak, was in my mother's hands. Observe her rushing, scissors in hand, thread in mouth, to the drawers where her daughters' Sabbath clothes were kept. Or go to church next Sunday, and watch a certain family filing in, the boy lifting his legs high to show off his new boots, but all the others demure, especially the timid, unobservant-looking little woman in the rear of them. If you were the minister's wife that day or the banker's daughters you would have got a shock. But she bought the christening robe, and when I used to ask why, she would beam and look conscious, and say she wanted to be extravagant once. And she told me, still smiling, that the more a woman was given to stitching and making things for herself, the greater was her passionate desire now and again to rush to the shops and "be foolish." The christening robe with its pathetic frills is over half a century old now, and has begun to droop a little, like a daisy whose time is past; but it is as fondly kept together as ever: I saw it in use again only the other day.

My mother lay in bed with the christening robe beside her, and I peeped in many times at the door and then went to the stair and sat on it and sobbed. I know not if it was that first day, or many days afterwards, that there came to me, my sister, the daughter my mother loved the best; yes, more I am sure even than she loved me, whose great glory she has been since I was six years old. This sister, who was then passing out of her 'teens, came to me with a very anxious face and wringing her hands, and she told me to go ben to my mother and say to her that she still had another boy. I went ben excitedly, but the room was dark, and when I heard the door shut and no sound come from the bed I was afraid, and I stood still. I suppose I was breathing hard, or perhaps I was crying, for after a time I heard a listless voice that had never been listless before say, "Is that you?" I think the tone hurt me, for I made no answer, and then the voice said more anxiously "Is that you?" again. I thought it was the dead boy she was speaking to, and I said in a little lonely voice, "No, it's no him, it's just me." Then I heard a cry, and my mother turned in bed, and though it was dark I knew that she was holding out her arms.

After that I sat a great deal in her bed trying to make her forget him, which was my crafty way of playing physician, and if I saw anyone out of doors do something that made the others laugh I immediately hastened to that dark room and did it before her. I suppose I was an odd little figure; I have been told that my anxiety to brighten her gave my face a strained look and put a tremor into the joke (I would stand on my head in the bed, my feet against the wall, and then cry excitedly, "Are you laughing, mother?")—and perhaps what made her laugh was something I was unconscious of, but she did laugh suddenly now and then, whereupon I screamed exultantly to that dear sister, who was ever in waiting, to come and see the sight, but by the time she came the soft face was wet again. Thus I was deprived of some of my glory, and I remember once only making her laugh before witnesses. I kept a record of her laughs on a piece of paper, a stroke for each, and it was my custom to show this proudly to the doctor every morning. There were five strokes the first time I slipped it into his hand, and when their meaning was explained to him he laughed so boisterously, that I cried, "I wish that was one of hers!" Then he was sympathetic, and asked me if my mother had seen the paper yet, and when I shook my head he said that if I showed it to her now and told her that these were her five laughs he thought I might win another. I had less confidence, but he was the mysterious man whom you ran for in the dead of night (you flung sand at his window to waken him, and if it was only toothache he extracted the tooth through the open window, but when it was something sterner he was with you in the dark square at once, like a man who slept in his topcoat), so I did as he bade me, and not only did she laugh then but again when I put the laugh down, so that though it was really one laugh with a tear in the middle I counted it as two.

It was doubtless that same sister who told me not to sulk when my mother lay thinking of him, but to try instead to get her to talk about him. I did not see how this could make her the merry mother she used to be, but I was told that if I could not do it nobody could, and this made me eager to begin. At first, they say, I was often jealous, stopping her fond memories with the cry, "Do you mind nothing about me?" but that did not last; its place was taken by an intense desire (again, I think, my sister must have breathed it into life) to become so like him that even my mother should not see the difference, and many and artful were the questions I put to that end. Then I practised in secret, but after a whole week had passed I was still rather like myself. He had such a cheery way of whistling, she had told me, it had always brightened her at her work to hear him whistling, and when he whistled he stood with his legs apart, and his hands in the pockets of his knickerbockers. I decided to trust to this, so one day after I had learned his whistle (every boy of enterprise invents a whistle of his own) from boys who had been his comrades, I secretly put on a suit of his clothes, dark grey they were, with little spots, and they fitted me many years afterwards, and thus disguised I slipped, unknown to the others, into my mother's room. Quaking, I doubt not, yet so pleased, I stood still until she saw me, and then—how it must have hurt her! "Listen!" I cried in a glow of triumph, and I stretched my legs wide apart and plunged my hands into the pockets of my knickerbockers, and began to whistle.

She lived twenty-nine years after his death, such active years until toward the end, that you never knew where she was unless you took hold of her, and though she was frail henceforth and ever growing frailer, her housekeeping again became famous, so that brides called as a matter of course to watch her ca'ming and sanding and stitching: there are old people still, one or two, to tell with wonder in their eyes how she could bake twenty-four bannocks in the hour, and not a chip in one of them. And how many she gave away, how much she gave away of all she had, and what pretty ways she had of giving it! Her face beamed and rippled with mirth as before, and her laugh that I had tried so hard to force came running home again. I have heard no such laugh as hers save from merry children; the laughter of most of us ages, and wears out with the body, but hers remained gleeful to the last, as if it were born afresh every morning. There was always something of the child in her, and her laugh was its voice, as eloquent of the past to me as was the christening robe to her. But I had not made her forget the bit of her that was dead; in those nine-and-twenty years he was not removed one day farther from her. Many a time she fell asleep speaking to him, and even while she slept her lips moved and she smiled as if he had come back to her, and when she woke he might vanish so suddenly that she started up bewildered and looked about her, and then said slowly, "My David's dead!" or perhaps he remained long enough to whisper why he must leave her now, and then she lay silent with filmy eyes. When I became a man and he was still a boy of thirteen, I wrote a little paper called "Dead this Twenty Years," which was about a similar tragedy in another woman's life, and it is the only thing I have written that she never spoke about, not even to that daughter she loved the best. No one ever spoke of it to her, or asked her if she had read it: one does not ask a mother if she knows that there is a little coffin in the house. She read many times the book in which it is printed, but when she came to that chapter she would put her hands to her heart or even over her ears.

II

What She had Been

What she had been, what I should be, these were the two great subjects between us in my boyhood, and while we discussed the one we were deciding the other, though neither of us knew it.

Before I reached my tenth year a giant entered my native place in the night, and we woke to find him in possession. He transformed it into a new town at a rate with which we boys only could keep up, for as fast as he built dams we made rafts to sail in them; he knocked down houses, and there we were crying "Pilly!" among the ruins; he dug trenches, and we jumped them; we had to be dragged by the legs from beneath his engines, he sunk wells, and in we went. But though there were never circumstances to which boys could not adapt themselves in half an hour, older folk are slower in the uptake, and I am sure they stood and gaped at the changes so suddenly being worked in our midst, and scarce knew their way home now in the dark. Where had been formerly but the click of the shuttle was soon the roar of "power," handlooms were pushed into a corner as a room is cleared for a dance; every morning at half-past five the town was wakened with a yell, and from a chimney-stack that rose high into our caller air the conqueror waved for evermore his flag of smoke. Another era had dawned, new customs, new fashions sprang into life, all as lusty as if they had been born at twenty-one; as quickly as two people may exchange seats, the daughter, till now but a knitter of stockings, became the breadwinner, he who had been the breadwinner sat down to the knitting of stockings: what had been yesterday a nest of weavers was today a town of girls.

I am not of those who would fling stones at the change; it is something, surely, that backs are no longer prematurely bent; you may no more look through dim panes of glass at the aged poor weaving tremulously for their little bit of ground in the cemetery. Rather are their working years too few now, not because they will it so but because it is with youth that the power-looms must be fed. Well, this teaches them to make provision, and they have the means as they never had before. Not in batches are boys now sent to college; the half-dozen a year have dwindled to one, doubtless because in these days they can begin to draw wages as they step out of their fourteenth year. Here assuredly there is loss, but all the losses would be but a pebble in a sea of gain were it not for this, that with so many of the family, young mothers among them, working in the factories, home life is not so beautiful as it was. So much of what is great in Scotland has sprung from the closeness of the family ties; it is there I sometimes fear that my country is being struck. That we are all being reduced to one dead level, that character abounds no more and life itself is less interesting, such things I have read, but I do not believe them. I have even seen them given as my reason for writing of a past time, and in that at least there is no truth. In our little town, which is a sample of many, life is as interesting, as pathetic, as joyous as ever it was; no group of weavers was better to look at or think about than the rivulet of winsome girls that overruns our streets everytime the sluice is raised, the comedy of summer evenings and winter firesides is played with the old zest and every window-blind is the curtain of a romance. Once the lights of a little town are lit, who could ever hope to tell all its story, or the story of a single wynd in it? And who looking at lighted windows needs to turn to books? The reason my books deal with the past instead of with the life I myself have known is simply this, that I soon grow tired of writing tales unless I can see a little girl, of whom my mother has told me, wandering confidently through the pages. Such a grip has her memory of her girlhood had upon me since I was a boy of six.

Those innumerable talks with her made her youth as vivid to me as my own, and so much more quaint, for, to a child, the oddest of things, and the most richly coloured picture-book, is that his mother was once a child also, and the contrast between what she is and what she was is perhaps the source of all humour. My mother's father, the one hero of her life, died nine years before I was born, and I remember this with bewilderment, so familiarly does the weather-beaten mason's figure rise before me from the old chair on which I was nursed and now write my books. On the surface he is as hard as the stone on which he chiselled, and his face is dyed red by its dust, he is rounded in the shoulders and a "hoast" hunts him ever; sooner or later that cough must carry him off, but until then it shall not keep him from the quarry, nor shall his chapped hands, as long as they can grasp the mell. It is a night of rain or snow, and my mother, the little girl in a pinafore who is already his housekeeper, has been many times to the door to look for him. At last he draws nigh, hoasting. Or I see him setting off to church, for he was a great "stoop" of the Auld Licht kirk, and his mouth is very firm now as if there were a case of discipline to face, but on his way home he is bowed with pity. Perhaps his little daughter who saw him so stern an hour ago does not understand why he wrestles so long in prayer tonight, or why when he rises from his knees he presses her to him with unwonted tenderness. Or he is in this chair repeating to her his favourite poem, "The Cameronian's Dream," and at the first lines so solemnly uttered,

"In a dream of the night I was wafted away,"

she screams with excitement, just as I screamed long afterwards when she repeated them in his voice to me. Or I watch, as from a window, while she sets off through the long parks to the distant place where he is at work, in her hand a flagon which contains his dinner. She is singing to herself and gleefully swinging the flagon, she jumps the burn and proudly measures the jump with her eye, but she never dallies unless she meets a baby, for she was so fond of babies that she must hug each one she met, but while she hugged them she also noted how their robes were cut, and afterwards made paper patterns, which she concealed jealously, and in the fulness of time her first robe for her eldest born was fashioned from one of these patterns, made when she was in her twelfth year.

She was eight when her mother's death made her mistress of the house and mother to her little brother, and from that time she scrubbed and mended and baked and sewed, and argued with the flesher about the quarter pound of beef and penny bone which provided dinner for two days (but if you think that this was poverty you don't know the meaning of the word), and she carried the water from the pump, and had her washing-days and her ironings and a stocking always on the wire for odd moments, and gossiped like a matron with the other women, and humoured the men with a tolerant smile—all these things she did as a matter of course, leaping joyful from bed in the morning because there was so much to do, doing it as thoroughly and sedately as if the brides were already due for a lesson, and then rushing out in a fit of childishness to play dumps or palaulays with others of her age. I see her frocks lengthening, though they were never very short, and the games given reluctantly up. The horror of my boyhood was that I knew a time would come when I also must give up the games, and how it was to be done I saw not (this agony still returns to me in dreams, when I catch myself playing marbles, and look on with cold displeasure); I felt that I must continue playing in secret, and I took this shadow to her, when she told me her own experience, which convinced us both that we were very like each other inside. She had discovered that work is the best fun after all, and I learned it in time, but have my lapses, and so had she.

I know what was her favourite costume when she was at the age that they make heroines of: it was a pale blue with a pale blue bonnet, the white ribbons of which tied aggravatingly beneath the chin, and when questioned about this garb she never admitted that she looked pretty in it, but she did say, with blushes too, that blue was her colour, and then she might smile, as at some memory, and begin to tell us about a man who—but it ended there with another smile which was longer in departing. She never said, indeed she denied strenuously, that she had led the men a dance, but again the smile returned, and came between us and full belief. Yes, she had her little vanities; when she got the Mizpah ring she did carry that finger in such a way that the most reluctant must see. She was very particular about her gloves, and hid her boots so that no other should put them on, and then she forgot their hiding-place, and had suspicions of the one who found them. A good way of enraging her was to say that her last year's bonnet would do for this year without alteration, or that it would defy the face of clay to count the number of her shawls. In one of my books there is a mother who is setting off with her son for the town to which he had been called as minister, and she pauses on the threshold to ask him anxiously if he thinks her bonnet "sets" her. A reviewer said she acted thus, not because she cared how she looked, but for the sake of her son. This, I remember, amused my mother very much.

I have seen many weary on-dings of snow, but the one I seem to recollect best occurred nearly twenty years before I was born. It was at the time of my mother's marriage to one who proved a most loving as he was always a well-loved husband, a man I am very proud to be able to call my father. I know not for how many days the snow had been falling, but a day came when the people lost heart and would make no more gullies through it, and by next morning to do so was impossible, they could not fling the snow high enough. Its back was against every door when Sunday came, and none ventured out save a valiant few, who buffeted their way into my mother's home to discuss her predicament, for unless she was "cried" in the church that day she might not be married for another week, and how could she be cried with the minister a field away and the church buried to the waist? For hours they talked, and at last some men started for the church, which was several hundred yards distant. Three of them found a window, and forcing a passage through it, cried the pair, and that is how it came about that my father and mother were married on the first of March.

That would be the end, I suppose, if it were a story, but to my mother it was only another beginning, and not the last. I see her bending over the cradle of her first-born, college for him already in her eye (and my father not less ambitious), and anon it is a girl who is in the cradle, and then another girl—already a tragic figure to those who know the end. I wonder if any instinct told my mother that the great day of her life was when she bore this child; what I am sure of is that from the first the child followed her with the most wistful eyes and saw how she needed help and longed to rise and give it. For of physical strength my mother had never very much; it was her spirit that got through the work, and in those days she was often so ill that the sand rained on the doctor's window, and men ran to and fro with leeches, and "she is in life, we can say no more" was the information for those who came knocking at the door. "I am sorrow to say," her father writes in an old letter now before me, "that Margaret is in a state that she was never so bad before in this world. Till Wednesday night she was in as poor a condition as you could think of to be alive. However, after bleeding, leeching, etc., the Dr. says this morning that he is better hoped now, but at present we can say no more but only she is alive and in the hands of Him in whose hands all our lives are. I can give you no adequate view of what my feelings are, indeed they are a burden too heavy for me and I cannot describe them. I look on my right and left hand and find no comfort, and if it were not for the rock that is higher than I my spirit would utterly fall, but blessed be His name who can comfort those that are cast down. O for more faith in His supporting grace in this hour of trial."

Then she is "on the mend," she may "thole thro'" if they take great care of her, "which we will be forward to do." The fourth child dies when but a few weeks old, and the next at two years. She was her grandfather's companion, and thus he wrote of her death, this stern, self-educated Auld Licht with the chapped hands:—

"I hope you received my last in which I spoke of Dear little Lydia being unwell. Now with deep sorrow I must tell you that yesterday I assisted in laying her dear remains in the lonely grave. She died at 7 o'clock on Wednesday evening, I suppose by the time you had got the letter. The Dr. did not think it was croup till late on Tuesday night, and all that Medical aid could prescribe was done, but the Dr. had no hope after he saw that the croup was confirmed, and hard indeed would the heart have been that would not have melted at seeing what the dear little creature suffered all Wednesday until the feeble frame was quite worn out. She was quite sensible till within 2 hours of her death, and then she sunk quite low till the vital spark fled, and all medicine that she got she took with the greatest readiness, as if apprehensive they would make her well. I cannot well describe my feelings on the occasion. I thought that the fountain-head of my tears had now been dried up, but I have been mistaken, for I must confess that the briny rivulets descended fast on my furrowed cheeks, she was such a winning Child, and had such a regard for me and always came and told me all her little things, and as she was now speaking, some of her little prattle was very taking, and the lively images of these things intrude themselves more into my mind than they should do, but there is allowance for moderate grief on such occasions. But when I am telling you of my own grief and sorrow, I know not what to say of the bereaved Mother, she hath not met with anything in this world before that hath gone so near the quick with her. She had no handling of the last one as she was not able at the time, for she only had her once in her arms, and her affections had not time to be so fairly entwined around her. I am much afraid that she will not soon if ever get over this trial. Although she was weakly before, yet she was pretty well recovered, but this hath not only affected her mind, but her body is so much affected that she is not well able to sit so long as her bed is making and hath scarcely tasted meat (i.e. food) since Monday night, and till sometime is elapsed we cannot say how she may be. There is none that is not a Parent themselves that can fully sympathise with one in such a state. David is much affected also, but it is not so well known on him, and the younger branches of the family are affected but it will be only momentary. But alas in all this vast ado, there is only the sorrow of the world which worketh death. O how gladdening would it be if we were in as great bitterness for sin as for the loss of a first-born. O how unfitted persons or families is for trials who knows not the divine art of casting all their cares upon the Lord, and what multitudes are there that when earthly comforts is taken away, may well say What have I more? all their delight is placed in someone thing or another in the world, and who can blame them for unwillingly parting with what they esteem their chief good? O that we were wise to lay up treasure for the time of need, for it is truly a solemn affair to enter the lists with the king of terrors. It is strange that the living lay the things so little to heart until they have to engage in that war where there is no discharge. O that my head were waters and mine eyes a fountain of tears that I might weep day and night for my own and others' stupidity in this great matter. O for grace to do everyday work in its proper time and to live above the tempting cheating train of earthly things. The rest of the family are moderately well. I have been for some days worse than I have been for 8 months past, but I may soon get better. I am in the same way I have often been in before, but there is no security for it always being so, for I know that it cannot be far from the time when I will be one of those that once were. I have no other news to send you, and as little heart for them. I hope you will take the earliest opportunity of writing that you can, and be particular as regards Margaret, for she requires consolation."

He died exactly a week after writing this letter, but my mother was to live for another forty-four years. And joys of a kind never shared in by him were to come to her so abundantly, so long drawn out that, strange as it would have seemed to him to know it, her fuller life had scarce yet begun. And with the joys were to come their sweet, frightened comrades pain and grief; again she was to be touched to the quick, again and again to be so ill that "she is in life, we can say no more," but still she had attendants very "forward" to help her, some of them unborn in her father's time.

She told me everything, and so my memories of our little red town are coloured by her memories. I knew it as it had been for generations, and suddenly I saw it change, and the transformation could not fail to strike a boy, for these first years are the most impressionable (nothing that happens after we are twelve matters very much); they are also the most vivid years when we look back, and more vivid the farther we have to look, until, at the end, what lies between bends like a hoop, and the extremes meet. But though the new town is to me a glass through which I look at the old, the people I see passing up and down these wynds, sitting, nightcapped, on their barrow-shafts, hobbling in their blacks to church on Sunday, are less those I saw in my childhood than their fathers and mothers who did these things in the same way when my mother was young. I cannot picture the place without seeing her, as a little girl, come to the door of a certain house and beat her bass against the gav'le-end, or there is a wedding tonight, and the carriage with the white-eared horse is sent for a maiden in pale blue, whose bonnet-strings tie beneath the chin.

III

WHAT I SHOULD BE

My mother was a great reader, and with ten minutes to spare before the starch was ready would begin the "Decline and Fall"— and finish it, too, that winter. Foreign words in the text annoyed her and made her bemoan her want of a classical education—she had only attended a Dame's school during some easy months—but she never passed the foreign words by until their meaning was explained to her, and when next she and they met it was as acquaintances, which I think was clever of her. One of her delights was to learn from me scraps of Horace, and then bring them into her conversation with "colleged men." I have come upon her in lonely places, such as the stair-head or the east room, muttering these quotations aloud to herself, and I well remember how she would say to the visitors, "Ay, ay, it's very true, Doctor, but as you know, 'Eheu fugaces, Postume, Postume, labuntur anni,'" or "Sal, Mr. So-and-so, my lassie is thriving well, but would it no' be more to the point to say, 'O matra pulchra filia pulchrior'?" which astounded them very much if she managed to reach the end without being flung, but usually she had a fit of laughing in the middle, and so they found her out.

Biography and exploration were her favourite reading, for choice the biography of men who had been good to their mothers, and she liked the explorers to be alive so that she could shudder at the thought of their venturing forth again; but though she expressed a hope that they would have the sense to stay at home henceforth, she gleamed with admiration when they disappointed her. In later days I had a friend who was an African explorer, and she was in two minds about him; he was one of the most engrossing of mortals to her, she admired him prodigiously, pictured him at the head of his caravan, now attacked by savages, now by wild beasts, and adored him for the uneasy hours he gave her, but she was also afraid that he wanted to take me with him, and then she thought he should be put down by law. Explorers' mothers also interested her very much; the books might tell her nothing about them, but she could create them for herself and wring her hands in sympathy with them when they had got no news of him for six months.

Yet there were times when she grudged him to them—as the day when he returned victorious. Then what was before her eyes was not the son coming marching home again but an old woman peering for him round the window curtain and trying not to look uplifted. The newspaper reports would be about the son, but my mother's comment was "She's a proud woman this night."

We read many books together when I was a boy, "Robinson Crusoe" being the first (and the second), and the "Arabian Nights" should have been the next, for we got it out of the library (a penny for three days), but on discovering that they were nights when we had paid for knights we sent that volume packing, and I have curled my lips at it ever since. "The Pilgrim's Progress" we had in the house (it was as common a possession as a dresser-head), and so enamoured of it was I that I turned our garden into sloughs of Despond, with pea-sticks to represent Christian on his travels and a buffet-stool for his burden, but when I dragged my mother out to see my handiwork she was scared, and I felt for days, with a certain elation, that I had been a dark character. Besides reading every book we could hire or borrow I also bought one now and again, and while buying (it was the occupation of weeks) I read, standing at the counter, most of the other books in the shop, which is perhaps the most exquisite way of reading. And I took in a magazine called "Sunshine," the most delicious periodical, I am sure, of any day. It cost a halfpenny or a penny a month, and always, as I fondly remember, had a continued tale about the dearest girl, who sold water-cress, which is a dainty not grown and I suppose never seen in my native town. This romantic little creature took such hold of my imagination that I cannot eat water-cress even now without emotion. I lay in bed wondering what she would be up to in the next number; I have lost trout because when they nibbled my mind was wandering with her; my early life was embittered by her not arriving regularly on the first of the month. I know not whether it was owing to her loitering on the way one month to an extent flesh and blood could not bear, or because we had exhausted the penny library, but on a day I conceived a glorious idea, or it was put into my head by my mother, then desirous of making progress with her new clouty hearthrug. The notion was nothing short of this, why should I not write the tales myself? I did write them—in the garret—but they by no means helped her to get on with her work, for when I finished a chapter I bounded downstairs to read it to her, and so short were the chapters, so ready was the pen, that I was back with new manuscript before another clout had been added to the rug. Authorship seemed, like her bannock-baking, to consist of running between two points. They were all tales of adventure (happiest is he who writes of adventure), no characters were allowed within if I knew their like in the flesh, the scene lay in unknown parts, desert islands, enchanted gardens, with knights (none of your nights) on black chargers, and round the first corner a lady selling water-cress.

At twelve or thereabout I put the literary calling to bed for a time, having gone to a school where cricket and football were more esteemed, but during the year before I went to the university, it woke up and I wrote great part of a three-volume novel. The publisher replied that the sum for which he would print it was a hundred and—however, that was not the important point (I had sixpence): where he stabbed us both was in writing that he considered me a "clever lady." I replied stiffly that I was a gentleman, and since then I have kept that manuscript concealed. I looked through it lately, and, oh, but it is dull! I defy anyone to read it.

The malignancy of publishers, however, could not turn me back. From the day on which I first tasted blood in the garret my mind was made up; there could be no hum-dreadful-drum profession for me; literature was my game. It was not highly thought of by those who wished me well. I remember being asked by two maiden ladies, about the time I left the university, what I was to be, and when I replied brazenly, "An author," they flung up their hands, and one exclaimed reproachfully, "And you an M.A.!" My mother's views at first were not dissimilar; for long she took mine jestingly as something I would grow out of, and afterwards they hurt her so that I tried to give them up. To be a minister—that she thought was among the fairest prospects, but she was a very ambitious woman, and sometimes she would add, half scared at her appetite, that there were ministers who had become professors, "but it was not canny to think of such things."

I had one person only on my side, an old tailor, one of the fullest men I have known, and quite the best talker. He was a bachelor (he told me all that is to be known about woman), a lean man, pallid of face, his legs drawn up when he walked as if he was ever carrying something in his lap; his walks were of the shortest, from the tea-pot on the hob to the board on which he stitched, from the board to the hob, and so to bed. He might have gone out had the idea struck him, but in the years I knew him, the last of his brave life, I think he was only in the open twice, when he "flitted"—changed his room for another hard by. I did not see him make these journeys, but I seem to see him now, and he is somewhat dizzy in the odd atmosphere; in one hand he carries a box-iron, he raises the other, wondering what this is on his head, it is a hat; a faint smell of singed cloth goes by with him. This man had heard of my set of photographs of the poets and asked for a sight of them, which led to our first meeting. I remember how he spread them out on his board, and after looking long at them, turned his gaze on me and said solemnly,

> *What can I do to be forever known,*
> *And make the age to come my own?*

These lines of Cowley were new to me, but the sentiment was not new, and I marvelled how the old tailor could see through me so well. So it was strange to me to discover presently that he had not been thinking of me at all, but of his own young days, when that couplet sang in his head, and he, too, had thirsted to set off for Grub Street, but was afraid, and while he hesitated old age came, and then Death, and found him grasping a box-iron.

I hurried home with the mouthful, but neighbours had dropped in, and this was for her ears only, so I drew her to the stair, and said imperiously,

> *What can I do to be forever known,*
> *And make the age to come my own?*

It was an odd request for which to draw her from a tea-table, and she must have been surprised, but I think she did not laugh, and in after years she would repeat the lines fondly, with a flush on her soft face. "That is the kind you would like to be yourself!" we would say in jest to her, and she would reply almost passionately, "No, but I would be windy of being his mother." It is possible that she could have been his mother had that other son lived, he might have managed it from sheer love of her, but for my part I can smile at one of those two figures on the stair now, having long given up the dream of being forever known, and seeing myself more akin to my friend, the tailor, for as he was found at the end on his board, so I hope shall I be found at my handloom, doing honestly the work that suits me best. Who should know so well as I that it is but a handloom compared to the great guns that reverberate through the age to come? But she who stood with me on the stair that day was a very simple woman, accustomed all her life to making the most of small things, and I weaved sufficiently well to please her, which has been my only steadfast ambition since I was a little boy.

Not less than mine became her desire that I should have my way— but, ah, the iron seats in that park of horrible repute, and that bare room at the top of many flights of stairs! While I was away at college she drained all available libraries for books about those who go to London to live by the pen, and they all told the same shuddering tale. London, which she never saw, was to her a monster that licked up country youths as they stepped from the train; there were the garrets in which they sat abject, and the park seats where they passed the night. Those park seats were the monster's glaring eyes to her, and as I go by them now she is nearer to me than when I am in any other part of London. I daresay that when night comes, this Hyde Park which is so gay by day, is haunted by the ghosts of many mothers, who run, wild-eyed, from seat to seat, looking for their sons.

But if we could dodge those dreary seats she longed to see me try my luck, and I sought to exclude them from the picture by drawing maps of London with Hyde Park left out. London was as strange to me as to her, but long before I was shot upon it I knew it by maps, and drew them more accurately than I could draw them now. Many a time she and I took our jaunt together through the map, and were most gleeful, popping into telegraph offices to wire my father and sister that we should not be home till late, winking to my books in lordly shop-windows, lunching at restaurants (and remembering not to call it dinner), saying, "How do?" to Mr. Alfred Tennyson when we passed him in Regent Street, calling at publishers' offices for cheque, when "Will you take care of it, or shall I?" I asked gaily, and she would be certain to reply, "I'm thinking we'd better take it to the bank and get the money," for she always felt surer of money than of cheques; so to the bank we went ("Two tens, and the rest in gold"), and thence straightway (by cab) to the place where you buy sealskin coats for middling old ladies. But ere the laugh was done the park would come through the map like a blot.

"If you could only be sure of as much as would keep body and soul together," my mother would say with a sigh.

"With something over, mother, to send to you."

"You couldna expect that at the start."

The wench I should have been courting now was journalism, that grisette of literature who has a smile and a hand for all beginners, welcoming them at the threshold, teaching them so much that is worth knowing, introducing them to the other lady whom they have worshipped from afar, showing them even how to woo her, and then bidding them a bright God-speed—he were an ingrate who, having had her joyous companionship, no longer flings her a kiss as they pass. But though she bears no ill-will when she is jilted, you must serve faithfully while you are hers, and you must seek her out and make much of her, and, until you can rely on her good-nature (note this), not a word about the other lady. When at last she took me in I grew so fond of her that I called her by the other's name, and even now I think at times that there was more fun in the little sister, but I began by wooing her with contributions that were all misfits. In an old book I find columns of notes about works projected at this time, nearly all to consist of essays on deeply uninteresting subjects; the lightest was to be a volume on the older satirists, beginning with Skelton and Tom Nash—the half of that manuscript still lies in a dusty chest—the only story was about Mary Queen of Scots, who was also the subject of many unwritten papers. Queen Mary seems to have been luring me to my undoing ever since I saw Holyrood, and I have a horrid fear that I may write that novel yet. That anything could be written about my native place never struck me. We had read somewhere that a novelist is better equipped than most of his trade if he knows himself and one woman, and my mother said, "You know yourself, for everybody must know himself" (there never was a woman who knew less about herself than she), and she would add dolefully, "But I doubt I'm the only woman you know well."

"Then I must make you my heroine," I said lightly.

"A gey auld-farrant-like heroine!" she said, and we both laughed at the notion—so little did we read the future.

Thus it is obvious what were my qualifications when I was rashly engaged as a leader-writer (it was my sister who saw the advertisement) on an English provincial paper. At the moment I was as uplifted as the others, for the chance had come at last, with what we all regarded as a prodigious salary, but I was wanted in the beginning of the week, and it suddenly struck me that the leaders were the one thing I had always skipped. Leaders! How were they written? what were they about? My mother was already sitting triumphant among my socks, and I durst not let her see me quaking. I retired to ponder, and presently she came to me with the daily paper. Which were the leaders? she wanted to know, so evidently I could get no help from her. Had she anymore newspapers? I asked, and after rummaging, she produced a few with which her boxes had been lined. Others, very dusty, came from beneath carpets, and lastly a sooty bundle was dragged down the chimney. Surrounded by these I sat down, and studied how to become a journalist.

IV

AN EDITOR

A devout lady, to whom some friend had presented one of my books, used to say when asked how she was getting on with it, "Sal, it's dreary, weary, uphill work, but I've wrastled through with tougher jobs in my time, and, please God, I'll wrastle through with this one." It was in this spirit, I fear, though she never told me so, that my mother wrestled for the next year or more with my leaders, and indeed I was always genuinely sorry for the people I saw reading them. In my spare hours I was trying journalism of another kind and sending it to London, but nearly eighteen months elapsed before there came to me, as unlooked for as a telegram, the thought that there was something quaint about my native place. A boy who found that a knife had been put into his pocket in the night could not have been more surprised. A few days afterwards I sent my mother a London evening paper with an article entitled "An Auld Licht Community," and they told me that when she saw the heading she laughed, because there was something droll to her in the sight of the words Auld Licht in print. For her, as for me, that newspaper was soon to have the face of a friend. To this day I never pass its placards in the street without shaking it by the hand, and she used to sew its pages together as lovingly as though they were a child's frock; but let the truth be told, when she read that first article she became alarmed, and fearing the talk of the town, hid the paper from all eyes. For sometime afterwards, while I proudly pictured her showing this and similar articles to all who felt an interest in me, she was really concealing them fearfully in a bandbox on the garret stair. And she wanted to know by return of post whether I was paid for these articles as much as I was paid for real articles; when she heard that I was paid better, she laughed again and had them out of the bandbox for re-reading, and it cannot be denied that she thought the London editor a fine fellow but slightly soft.

When I sent off that first sketch I thought I had exhausted the subject, but our editor wrote that he would like something more of the same, so I sent him a marriage, and he took it, and then I tried him with a funeral, and he took it, and really it began to look as if we had him. Now my mother might have been discovered, in answer to certain excited letters, flinging the bundle of undarned socks from her lap, and "going in for literature"; she was racking her brains, by request, for memories I might convert into articles, and they came to me in letters which she dictated to my sisters. How well I could hear her sayings between the lines: "But the editor-man will never stand that, it's perfect blethers"—"By this post it must go, I tell you; we must take the editor when he's hungry—we canna be blamed for it, can we? he prints them of his free will, so the wite is his"—"But I'm near terrified.—If London folk reads them we're done for." And I was sounded as to the advisability of sending him a present of a lippie of shortbread, which was to be her crafty way of getting round him. By this time, though my mother and I were hundreds of miles apart, you may picture us waving our hands to each other across country, and shouting "Hurrah!" You may also picture the editor in his office thinking he was behaving like a shrewd man of business, and unconscious that up in the north there was an elderly lady chuckling so much at him that she could scarcely scrape the potatoes.

I was now able to see my mother again, and the park seats no longer loomed so prominent in our map of London. Still, there they were, and it was with an effort that she summoned up courage to let me go. She feared changes, and who could tell that the editor would continue to be kind? Perhaps when he saw me—

She seemed to be very much afraid of his seeing me, and this, I would point out, was a reflection on my appearance or my manner.

No, what she meant was that I looked so young, and—and that would take him aback, for had I not written as an aged man?

"But he knows my age, mother."

"I'm glad of that, but maybe he wouldna like you when he saw you."

"Oh, it is my manner, then!"

"I dinna say that, but—"

Here my sister would break in: "The short and the long of it is just this, she thinks nobody has such manners as herself. Can you deny it, you vain woman?" My mother would deny it vigorously.

"You stand there," my sister would say with affected scorn, "and tell me you don't think you could get the better of that man quicker than any of us?"

"Sal, I'm thinking I could manage him," says my mother, with a chuckle.

"How would you set about it?"

Then my mother would begin to laugh. "I would find out first if he had a family, and then I would say they were the finest family in London."

"Yes, that is just what you would do, you cunning woman! But if he has no family?"

"I would say what great men editors are!"

"He would see through you."

"Not he!"

"You don't understand that what imposes on common folk would never hoodwink an editor."

"That's where you are wrong. Gentle or simple, stupid or clever, the men are all alike in the hands of a woman that flatters them."

"Ah, I'm sure there are better ways of getting round an editor than that."

"I daresay there are," my mother would say with conviction, "but if you try that plan you will never need to try another."

"How artful you are, mother—you with your soft face! Do you not think shame?"

"Pooh!" says my mother brazenly.

"I can see the reason why you are so popular with men."

"Ay, you can see it, but they never will."

"Well, how would you dress yourself if you were going to that editor's office?"

"Of course I would wear my silk and my Sabbath bonnet."

"It is you who are shortsighted now, mother. I tell you, you would manage him better if you just put on your old grey shawl and one of your bonny white mutches, and went in half smiling and half timid and said, 'I am the mother of him that writes about the Auld Lichts, and I want you to promise that he will never have to sleep in the open air.'"

But my mother would shake her head at this, and reply almost hotly, "I tell you if I ever go into that man's office, I go in silk."

I wrote and asked the editor if I should come to London, and he said No, so I went, laden with charges from my mother to walk in the middle of the street (they jump out on you as you are turning a corner), never to venture forth after sunset, and always to lock up everything (I who could never lock up anything, except my heart in company). Thanks to this editor, for the others would have nothing to say to me though I battered on all their doors, she was soon able to sleep at nights without the dread that I should be waking presently with the iron-work of certain seats figured on my person, and what relieved her very much was that I had begun to write as if Auld Lichts were not the only people I knew of. So long as I confined myself to them she had a haunting fear that, even though the editor remained blind to his best interests, something would one day go crack within me (as the mainspring of a watch breaks) and my pen refuse to write for evermore. "Ay, I like the article brawly," she would say timidly, "but I'm doubting it's the last—I always have a sort of terror the new one may be the last," and if many days elapsed before the arrival of another article her face would say mournfully, "The blow has fallen—he can think of nothing more to write about." If I ever shared her fears I never told her so, and the articles that were not Scotch grew in number until there were hundreds of them, all carefully preserved by her: they were the only thing in the house that, having served one purpose, she did not convert into something else, yet they could give her uneasy moments. This was because I nearly always assumed a character when I wrote; I must be a country squire, or an undergraduate, or a butler, or a member of the House of Lords, or a dowager, or a lady called Sweet Seventeen, or an engineer in India, else was my pen clogged, and though this gave my mother certain fearful joys, causing her to laugh unexpectedly (so far as my articles were concerned she nearly always laughed in the wrong place), it also scared her. Much to her amusement the editor continued to prefer the Auld Licht papers, however, as was proved (to those who knew him) by his way of thinking that the others would pass as they were, while he sent these back and asked me to make them better. Here again she came to my aid. I had said that the row of stockings were hung on a string by the fire, which was a recollection of my own, but she could tell me whether they were hung upside down. She became quite skilful at sending or giving me (for now I could be with her half the year) the right details, but still she smiled at the editor, and in her gay moods she would say, "I was fifteen when I got my first pair of elastic-sided boots. Tell him my charge for this important news is two pounds ten."

"Ay, but though we're doing well, it's no' the same as if they were a book with your name on it." So the ambitious woman would say with a sigh, and I did my best to turn the Auld Licht sketches into a book with my name on it. Then perhaps we understood most fully how good a friend our editor had been, for just as I had been able to find no well-known magazine—and I think I tried all—which would print any article or story about the poor of my native land, so now the publishers, Scotch and English, refused to accept the book as a gift. I was willing to present it to them, but they would have it in no guise; there seemed to be a blight on everything that was Scotch. I daresay we sighed, but never were collaborators more prepared for rejection, and though my mother might look wistfully at the scorned manuscript at times and murmur, "You poor cold little crittur shut away in a drawer, are you dead or just sleeping?" she had still her editor to say grace over. And at last publishers, sufficiently daring and far more than sufficiently generous, were found for us by a dear friend, who made one woman very "uplifted." He also was an editor, and had as large a part in making me a writer of books as the other in determining what the books should be about.

Now that I was an author I must get into a club. But you should have heard my mother on clubs! She knew of none save those to which you subscribe a pittance weekly in anticipation of rainy days, and the London clubs were her scorn. Often I heard her on them—she raised her voice to make me hear, whichever room I might be in, and it was when she was sarcastic that I skulked the most: "Thirty pounds is what he will have to pay the first year, and ten pounds a year after that. You think it's a lot o' siller? Oh no, you're mista'en—it's nothing ava. For the third part of thirty pounds you could rent a four-roomed house, but what is a four-roomed house, what is thirty pounds, compared to the glory of being a member of a club? Where does the glory come in? Sal, you needna ask me, I'm just a doited auld stock that never set foot in a club, so it's little I ken about glory. But I may tell you if you bide in London and canna become member of a club, the best you can do is to tie a rope round your neck and slip out of the world. What use are they? Oh, they're terrible useful. You see it doesna do for a man in London to eat his dinner in his lodgings. Other men shake their heads at him. He maun away to his club if he is to be respected. Does he get good dinners at the club? Oh, they cow! You get no common beef at clubs; there is a manzy of different things all sauced up to be unlike themsels. Even the potatoes daurna look like potatoes. If the food in a club looks like what it is, the members run about, flinging up their hands and crying, 'Woe is me!' Then this is another thing, you get your letters sent to the club instead of to your lodgings. You see you would get them sooner at your lodgings, and you may have to trudge weary miles to the club for them, but that's a great advantage, and cheap at thirty pounds, is it no'? I wonder they can do it at the price."

My wisest policy was to remain downstairs when these withering blasts were blowing, but probably I went up in self-defence.

"I never saw you so pugnacious before, mother."

"Oh," she would reply promptly, "you canna expect me to be sharp in the uptake when I am no' a member of a club."

"But the difficulty is in becoming a member. They are very particular about whom they elect, and I daresay I shall not get in."

"Well, I'm but a poor crittur (not being member of a club), but I think I can tell you to make your mind easy on that head. You'll get in, I'se uphaud—and your thirty pounds will get in, too."

"If I get in it will be because the editor is supporting me."

"It's the first ill thing I ever heard of him."

"You don't think he is to get any of the thirty pounds, do you?"

"'Deed if I did I should be better pleased, for he has been a good friend to us, but what maddens me is that every penny of it should go to those bare-faced scoundrels."

"What bare-faced scoundrels?"

"Them that have the club."

"But all the members have the club between them."

"Havers! I'm no' to be catched with chaff."

"But don't you believe me?"

"I believe they've filled your head with their stories till you swallow whatever they tell you. If the place belongs to the members, why do they have to pay thirty pounds?"

"To keep it going."

"They dinna have to pay for their dinners, then?"

"Oh yes, they have to pay extra for dinner."

"And a gey black price, I'm thinking."

"Well, five or six shillings."

"Is that all? Losh, it's nothing, I wonder they dinna raise the price."

Nevertheless my mother was of a sex that scorned prejudice, and, dropping sarcasm, she would at times cross-examine me as if her mind was not yet made up. "Tell me this, if you were to fall ill, would you be paid a weekly allowance out of the club?"

No, it was not that kind of club.

"I see. Well, I am just trying to find out what kind of club it is. Do you get anything out of it for accidents?"

Not a penny.

"Anything at New Year's time?"

Not so much as a goose.

"Is there anyone mortal thing you get free out of that club?"

There was not one mortal thing.

"And thirty pounds is what you pay for this?"

If the committee elected me.

"How many are in the committee?"

About a dozen, I thought.

"A dozen! Ay, ay, that makes two pound ten apiece."

When I was elected I thought it wisdom to send my sister upstairs with the news. My mother was ironing, and made no comment, unless with the iron, which I could hear rattling more violently in its box. Presently I heard her laughing—at me undoubtedly, but she had recovered control over her face before she came downstairs to congratulate me sarcastically. This was grand news, she said without a twinkle, and I must write and thank the committee, the noble critturs. I saw behind her mask, and maintained a dignified silence, but she would have another shot at me. "And tell them," she said from the door, "you were doubtful of being elected, but your auld mother had aye a mighty confidence they would snick you in." I heard her laughing softly as she went up the stair, but though I had provided her with a joke I knew she was burning to tell the committee what she thought of them.

Money, you see, meant so much to her, though even at her poorest she was the most cheerful giver. In the old days, when the article arrived, she did not read it at once, she first counted the lines to discover what we should get for it—she and the daughter who was so dear to her had calculated the payment per line, and I remember once overhearing a discussion between them about whether that sub-title meant another sixpence. Yes, she knew the value of money; she had always in the end got the things she wanted, but now she could get them more easily, and it turned her simple life into a fairy tale. So often in those days she went down suddenly upon her knees; we would come upon her thus, and go away noiselessly. After her death I found that she had preserved in a little box, with a photograph of me as a child, the envelopes which had contained my first cheques. There was a little ribbon round them.

V

A Day of Her Life

I should like to call back a day of her life as it was at this time, when her spirit was as bright as ever and her hand as eager, but she was no longer able to do much work. It should not be difficult, for she repeated herself from day to day and yet did it with a quaint unreasonableness that was ever yielding fresh delight. Our love for her was such that we could easily tell what she would do in given circumstances, but she had always a new way of doing it.

Well, with break of day she wakes and sits up in bed and is standing in the middle of the room. So nimble was she in the mornings (one of our troubles with her) that these three actions must be considered as one; she is on the floor before you have time to count them. She has strict orders not to rise until her fire is lit, and having broken them there is a demure elation on her face. The question is what to do before she is caught and hurried to bed again. Her fingers are tingling to prepare the breakfast; she would dearly love to black-lead the grate, but that might rouse her daughter from whose side she has slipped so cunningly. She catches sight of the screen at the foot of the bed, and immediately her soft face becomes very determined. To guard her from draughts the screen had been brought here from the lordly east room, where it was of no use whatever. But in her opinion it was too beautiful for use; it belonged to the east room, where she could take pleasant peeps at it; she had objected to its removal, even become low-spirited. Now is her opportunity. The screen is an unwieldy thing, but still as a mouse she carries it, and they are well under weigh when it strikes against the gas-bracket in the passage. Next moment a reproachful hand arrests her. She is challenged with being out of bed, she denies it—standing in the passage. Meekly or stubbornly she returns to bed, and it is no satisfaction to you that you can say, "Well, well, of all the women!" and so on, or "Surely you knew that the screen was brought here to protect you," for she will reply scornfully, "Who was touching the screen?"

By this time I have wakened (I am through the wall) and join them anxiously: so often has my mother been taken ill in the night that the slightest sound from her room rouses the house. She is in bed again, looking as if she had never been out of it, but I know her and listen sternly to the tale of her misdoings. She is not contrite. Yes, maybe she did promise not to venture forth on the cold floors of daybreak, but she had risen for a moment only, and we just t'neaded her with our talk about draughts—there were no such things as draughts in her young days—and it is more than she can do (here she again attempts to rise but we hold her down) to lie there and watch that beautiful screen being spoilt. I reply that the beauty of the screen has ever been its miserable defect: ho, there! for a knife with which to spoil its beauty and make the bedroom its fitting home. As there is no knife handy, my foot will do; I raise my foot, and then—she sees that it is bare, she cries to me excitedly to go back to bed lest I catch cold. For though, ever careless of herself, she will wander the house unshod, and tell us not to talk havers when we chide her, the sight of one of us similarly negligent rouses her anxiety at once. She is willing now to sign any vow if only I will take my bare feet back to bed, but probably she is soon after me in hers to make sure that I am nicely covered up.

It is scarcely six o'clock, and we have all promised to sleep for another hour, but in ten minutes she is sure that eight has struck (house disgraced), or that if it has not, something is wrong with the clock. Next moment she is captured on her way downstairs to wind up the clock. So evidently we must be up and doing, and as we have no servant, my sister disappears into the kitchen, having first asked me to see that "that woman" lies still, and "that woman" calls out that she always does lie still, so what are we blethering about?

She is up now, and dressed in her thick maroon wrapper; over her shoulders (lest she should stray despite our watchfulness) is a shawl, not placed there by her own hands, and on her head a delicious mutch. O that I could sing the pæan of the white mutch (and the dirge of the elaborate black cap) from the day when she called witchcraft to her aid and made it out of snow-flakes, and the dear worn hands that washed it tenderly in a basin, and the starching of it, and the finger-iron for its exquisite frills that looked like curls of sugar, and the sweet bands with which it tied beneath the chin! The honoured snowy mutch, how I love to see it smiling to me from the doors and windows of the poor; it is always smiling—sometimes maybe a wavering wistful smile, as if a tear-drop lay hidden among, the frills. A hundred times I have taken the characterless cap from my mother's head and put the mutch in its place and tied the bands beneath her chin, while she protested but was well pleased. For in her heart she knew what suited her best and would admit it, beaming, when I put a mirror into her hands and told her to look; but nevertheless the cap cost no less than so-and-so, whereas— Was that a knock at the door? She is gone, to put on her cap!

She begins the day by the fireside with the New Testament in her hands, an old volume with its loose pages beautifully refixed, and its covers sewn and resewn by her, so that you would say it can never fall to pieces. It is mine now, and to me the black threads with which she stitched it are as part of the contents. Other books she read in the ordinary manner, but this one differently, her lips moving with each word as if she were reading aloud, and her face very solemn. The Testament lies open on her lap long after she has ceased to read, and the expression of her face has not changed.

I have seen her reading other books early in the day but never without a guilty look on her face, for she thought reading was scarce respectable until night had come. She spends the forenoon in what she calls doing nothing, which may consist in stitching so hard that you would swear she was an over-worked seamstress at it for her life, or you will find her on a table with nails in her mouth, and anon she has to be chased from the garret (she has suddenly decided to change her curtains), or she is under the bed searching for band-boxes and asking sternly where we have put that bonnet. On the whole she is behaving in a most exemplary way today (not once have we caught her trying to go out into the washing-house), and we compliment her at dinner-time, partly because she deserves it, and partly to make her think herself so good that she will eat something, just to maintain her new character. I question whether one hour of all her life was given to thoughts of food; in her great days to eat seemed to her to be waste of time, and afterwards she only ate to boast of it, as something she had done to please us. She seldom remembered whether she had dined, but always presumed she had, and while she was telling me in all good faith what the meal consisted of, it might be brought in. When in London I had to hear daily what she was eating, and perhaps she had refused all dishes until they produced the pen and ink. These were flourished before her, and then she would say with a sigh, "Tell him I am to eat an egg." But they were not so easily deceived; they waited, pen in hand, until the egg was eaten.

She never "went for a walk" in her life. Many long trudges she had as a girl when she carried her father's dinner in a flagon to the country place where he was at work, but to walk with no end save the good of your health seemed a very droll proceeding to her. In her young days, she was positive, no one had ever gone for a walk, and she never lost the belief that it was an absurdity introduced by a new generation with too much time on their hands. That they enjoyed it she could not believe; it was merely a form of showing off, and as they passed her window she would remark to herself with blasting satire, "Ay, Jeames, are you off for your walk?" and add fervently, "Rather you than me!" I was one of those who walked, and though she smiled, and might drop a sarcastic word when she saw me putting on my boots, it was she who had heated them in preparation for my going. The arrangement between us was that she should lie down until my return, and to ensure its being carried out I saw her in bed before I started, but with the bang of the door she would be at the window to watch me go: there is one spot on the road where a thousand times I have turned to wave my stick to her, while she nodded and smiled and kissed her hand to me. That kissing of the hand was the one English custom she had learned.

In an hour or so I return, and perhaps find her in bed, according to promise, but still I am suspicious. The way to her detection is circuitous.

"I'll need to be rising now," she says, with a yawn that may be genuine.

"How long have you been in bed?"

"You saw me go."

"And then I saw you at the window. Did you go straight back to bed?"

"Surely I had that much sense."

"The truth!"

"I might have taken a look at the clock first."

"It is a terrible thing to have a mother who prevaricates. Have you been lying down ever since I left?"

"Thereabout."

"What does that mean exactly?"

"Off and on."

"Have you been to the garret?"

"What should I do in the garret?"

"But have you?"

"I might just have looked up the garret stair."

"You have been redding up the garret again!"

"Not what you could call a redd up."

"O, woman, woman, I believe you have not been in bed at all!"

"You see me in it."

"My opinion is that you jumped into bed when you heard me open the door."

"Havers."

"Did you?"

"No."

"Well, then, when you heard me at the gate?"

"It might have been when I heard you at the gate."

As daylight goes she follows it with her sewing to the window, and gets another needleful out of it, as one may run after a departed visitor for a last word, but now the gas is lit, and no longer is it shameful to sit down to literature. If the book be a story by George Eliot or Mrs. Oliphant, her favourites (and mine) among women novelists, or if it be a Carlyle, and we move softly, she will read, entranced, for hours. Her delight in Carlyle was so well known that various good people would send her books that contained a page about him; she could place her finger on any passage wanted in the biography as promptly as though she were looking for some article in her own drawer, and given a date she was often able to tell you what they were doing in Cheyne Row that day. Carlyle, she decided, was not so much an ill man to live with as one who needed a deal of managing, but when I asked if she thought she could have managed him she only replied with a modest smile that meant "Oh no!" but had the face of "Sal, I would have liked to try."

One lady lent her some scores of Carlyle letters that have never been published, and crabbed was the writing, but though my mother liked to have our letters read aloud to her, she read everyone of these herself, and would quote from them in her talk. Side by side with the Carlyle letters, which show him in his most gracious light, were many from his wife to a friend, and in one of these a romantic adventure is described—I quote from memory, and it is a poor memory compared to my mother's, which registered everything by a method of her own: "What might be the age of Bell Tibbits? Well, she was born the week I bought the boiler, so she'll be one-and-fifty (no less!) come Martinmas." Mrs. Carlyle had got into the train at a London station and was feeling very lonely, for the journey to Scotland lay before her and no one had come to see her off. Then, just as the train was starting, a man jumped into the carriage, to her regret until she saw his face, when, behold, they were old friends, and the last time they met (I forget how many years before) he had asked her to be his wife. He was very nice, and if I remember aright, saw her to her journey's end, though he had intended to alight at some half-way place. I call this an adventure, and I am sure it seemed to my mother to be the most touching and memorable adventure that can come into a woman's life. "You see he hadna forgot," she would say proudly, as if this was a compliment in which all her sex could share, and on her old tender face shone some of the elation with which Mrs. Carlyle wrote that letter.

But there were times, she held, when Carlyle must have made his wife a glorious woman. "As when?" I might inquire.

"When she keeked in at his study door and said to herself, 'The whole world is ringing with his fame, and he is my man!'"

"And then," I might point out, "he would roar to her to shut the door."

"Pooh!" said my mother, "a man's roar is neither here nor there." But her verdict as a whole was, "I would rather have been his mother than his wife."

So we have got her into her chair with the Carlyles, and all is well. Furthermore, "to mak siccar," my father has taken the opposite side of the fireplace and is deep in the latest five columns of Gladstone, who is his Carlyle. He is to see that she does not slip away fired by a conviction, which suddenly overrides her pages, that the kitchen is going to rack and ruin for want of her, and she is to recall him to himself should he put his foot in the fire and keep it there, forgetful of all save his hero's eloquence. (We were a family who needed a deal of watching.) She is not interested in what Mr. Gladstone has to say; indeed she could never be brought to look upon politics as of serious concern for grown folk (a class in which she scarcely included man), and she gratefully gave up reading "leaders" the day I ceased to write them. But like want of reasonableness, a love for having the last word, want of humour and the like, politics were in her opinion a mannish attribute to be tolerated, and Gladstone was the name of the something which makes all our sex such queer characters. She had a profound faith in him as an aid to conversation, and if there were silent men in the company would give him to them to talk about, precisely as she divided a cake among children. And then, with a motherly smile, she would leave them to gorge on him. But in the idolising of Gladstone she recognised, nevertheless, a certain inevitability, and would no more have tried to contend with it than to sweep a shadow off the floor. Gladstone was, and there was an end of it in her practical philosophy. Nor did she accept him coldly; like a true woman she sympathised with those who suffered severely, and they knew it and took counsel of her in the hour of need. I remember one ardent Gladstonian who, as a general election drew near, was in sore straits indeed, for he disbelieved in Home Rule, and yet how could he vote against "Gladstone's man"? His distress was so real that it gave him a hang-dog appearance. He put his case gloomily before her, and until the day of the election she riddled him with sarcasm; I think he only went to her because he found a mournful enjoyment in seeing a false Gladstonian tortured.

It was all such plain-sailing for him, she pointed out; he did not like this Home Rule, and therefore he must vote against it.

She put it pitiful clear, he replied with a groan.

But she was like another woman to him when he appeared before her on his way to the polling-booth.

"This is a watery Sabbath to you, I'm thinking," she said sympathetically, but without dropping her wires—for Home Rule or no Home Rule that stocking-foot must be turned before twelve o'clock.

A watery Sabbath means a doleful day, and "A watery Sabbath it is," he replied with feeling. A silence followed, broken only by the click of the wires. Now and again he would mutter, "Ay, well, I'll be going to vote—little did I think the day would come," and so on, but if he rose it was only to sit down again, and at last she crossed over to him and said softly, (no sarcasm in her voice now), "Away with you, and vote for Gladstone's man!" He jumped up and made off without a word, but from the east window we watched him strutting down the brae. I laughed, but she said, "I'm no sure that it's a laughing matter," and afterwards, "I would have liked fine to be that Gladstone's mother."

It is nine o'clock now, a quarter-past nine, half-past nine—all the same moment to me, for I am at a sentence that will not write. I know, though I can't hear, what my sister has gone upstairs to say to my mother:—

"I was in at him at nine, and he said, 'In five minutes,' so I put the steak on the brander, but I've been in thrice since then, and everytime he says, 'In five minutes,' and when I try to take the table-cover off, he presses his elbows hard on it, and growls. His supper will be completely spoilt."

"Oh, that weary writing!"

"I can do no more, mother, so you must come down and stop him."

"I have no power over him," my mother says, but she rises smiling, and presently she is opening my door.

"In five minutes!" I cry, but when I see that it is she I rise and put my arm round her. "What a full basket!" she says, looking at the waste-paper basket, which contains most of my work of the night and with a dear gesture she lifts up a torn page and kisses it. "Poor thing," she says to it, "and you would have liked so fine to be printed!" and she puts her hand over my desk to prevent my writing more.

"In the last five minutes," I begin, "one can often do more than in the first hour."

"Many a time I've said it in my young days," she says slowly.

"And proved it, too!" cries a voice from the door, the voice of one who was prouder of her even than I; it is true, and yet almost unbelievable, that anyone could have been prouder of her than I.

"But those days are gone," my mother says solemnly, "gone to come back no more. You'll put by your work now, man, and have your supper, and then you'll come up and sit beside your mother for a whiley, for soon you'll be putting her away in the kirk-yard."

I hear such a little cry from near the door.

So my mother and I go up the stair together. "We have changed places," she says; "that was just how I used to help you up, but I'm the bairn now."

She brings out the Testament again; it was always lying within reach; it is the lock of hair she left me when she died. And when she has read for a long time she "gives me a look," as we say in the north, and I go out, to leave her alone with God. She had been but a child when her mother died, and so she fell early into the way of saying her prayers with no earthly listener. Often and often I have found her on her knees, but I always went softly away, closing the door. I never heard her pray, but I know very well how she prayed, and that, when that door was shut, there was not a day in God's sight between the worn woman and the little child.

VI

Her Maid of All Work

A nd sometimes I was her maid of all work.

It is early morn, and my mother has come noiselessly into my room. I know it is she, though my eyes are shut, and I am only half awake. Perhaps I was dreaming of her, for I accept her presence without surprise, as if in the awakening I had but seen her go out at one door to come in at another. But she is speaking to herself.

"I'm sweer to waken him—I doubt he was working late—oh, that weary writing—no, I maunna waken him."

I start up. She is wringing her hands. "What is wrong?" I cry, but I know before she answers. My sister is down with one of the headaches against which even she cannot fight, and my mother, who bears physical pain as if it were a comrade, is most woebegone when her daughter is the sufferer. "And she winna let me go down the stair to make a cup of tea for her," she groans.

"I will soon make the tea, mother."

"Will you?" she says eagerly. It is what she has come to me for, but "It is a pity to rouse you," she says.

"And I will take charge of the house today, and light the fires and wash the dishes—"

"Na, oh no; no, I couldna ask that of you, and you an author."

"It won't be the first time, mother, since I was an author."

"More like the fiftieth!" she says almost gleefully, so I have begun well, for to keep up her spirits is the great thing today.

Knock at the door. It is the baker. I take in the bread, looking so sternly at him that he dare not smile.

Knock at the door. It is the postman. (I hope he did not see that I had the lid of the kettle in my other hand.)

Furious knocking in a remote part. This means that the author is in the coal cellar.

Anon I carry two breakfasts upstairs in triumph. I enter the bedroom like no mere humdrum son, but after the manner of the Glasgow waiter. I must say more about him. He had been my mother's one waiter, the only manservant she ever came in contact with, and they had met in a Glasgow hotel which she was eager to see, having heard of the monstrous things, and conceived them to resemble country inns with another twelve bedrooms. I remember how she beamed—yet tried to look as if it was quite an ordinary experience—when we alighted at the hotel door, but though she said nothing I soon read disappointment in her face. She knew how I was exulting in having her there, so would not say a word to damp me, but I craftily drew it out of her. No, she was very comfortable, and the house was grand beyond speech, but—but— where was he? he had not been very hearty. "He" was the landlord; she had expected him to receive us at the door and ask if we were in good health and how we had left the others, and then she would have asked him if his wife was well and how many children they had, after which we should all have sat down together to dinner. Two chambermaids came into her room and prepared it without a single word to her about her journey or on any other subject, and when they had gone, "They are two haughty misses," said my mother with spirit. But what she most resented was the waiter with his swagger black suit and short quick steps and the "towel" over his arm. Without so much as a "Welcome to Glasgow!" he showed us to our seats, not the smallest acknowledgment of our kindness in giving such munificent orders did we draw from him, he hovered around the table as if it would be unsafe to leave us with his knives and forks (he should have seen her knives and forks), when we spoke to each other he affected not to hear, we might laugh but this uppish fellow would not join in. We retired, crushed, and he had the final impudence to open the door for us. But though this hurt my mother at the time, the humour of our experiences filled her on reflection, and in her own house she would describe them with unction, sometimes to those who had been in many hotels, often to others who had been in none, and whoever were her listeners she made them laugh, though not always at the same thing.

So now when I enter the bedroom with the tray, on my arm is that badge of pride, the towel; and I approach with prim steps to inform Madam that breakfast is ready, and she puts on the society manner and addresses me as "Sir," and asks with cruel sarcasm for what purpose (except to boast) I carry the towel, and I say "Is there anything more I can do for Madam?" and Madam replies that there is one more thing I can do, and that is, eat her breakfast for her. But of this I take no notice, for my object is to fire her with the spirit of the game, so that she eats unwittingly.

Now that I have washed up the breakfast things I should be at my writing, and I am anxious to be at it, as I have an idea in my head, which, if it is of any value, has almost certainly been put there by her. But dare I venture? I know that the house has not been properly set going yet, there are beds to make, the exterior of the teapot is fair, but suppose someone were to look inside? What a pity I knocked over the flour-barrel! Can I hope that for once my mother will forget to inquire into these matters? Is my sister willing to let disorder reign until tomorrow? I determine to risk it. Perhaps I have been at work for half an hour when I hear movements overhead. One or other of them is wondering why the house is so quiet. I rattle the tongs, but even this does not satisfy them, so back into the desk go my papers, and now what you hear is not the scrape of a pen but the rinsing of pots and pans, or I am making beds, and making them thoroughly, because after I am gone my mother will come (I know her) and look suspiciously beneath the coverlet.

The kitchen is now speckless, not an unwashed platter in sight, unless you look beneath the table. I feel that I have earned time for an hour's writing at last, and at it I go with vigour. One page, two pages, really I am making progress, when—was that a door opening? But I have my mother's light step on the brain, so I "yoke" again, and next moment she is beside me. She has not exactly left her room, she gives me to understand; but suddenly a conviction had come to her that I was writing without a warm mat at my feet. She carries one in her hands. Now that she is here she remains for a time, and though she is in the arm-chair by the fire, where she sits bolt upright (she loved to have cushions on the unused chairs, but detested putting her back against them), and I am bent low over my desk, I know that contentment and pity are struggling for possession of her face: contentment wins when she surveys her room, pity when she looks at me. Every article of furniture, from the chairs that came into the world with me and have worn so much better, though I was new and they were second-hand, to the mantle-border of fashionable design which she sewed in her seventieth year, having picked up the stitch in half a lesson, has its story of fight and attainment for her, hence her satisfaction; but she sighs at sight of her son, dipping and tearing, and chewing the loathly pen.

"Oh, that weary writing!"

In vain do I tell her that writing is as pleasant to me as ever was the prospect of a tremendous day's ironing to her; that (to some, though not to me) new chapters are as easy to turn out as new bannocks. No, she maintains, for one bannock is the marrows of another, while chapters— and then, perhaps, her eyes twinkle, and says she saucily, "But, sal, you may be right, for sometimes your bannocks are as alike as mine!"

Or I may be roused from my writing by her cry that I am making strange faces again. It is my contemptible weakness that if I say a character smiled vacuously, I must smile vacuously; if he frowns or leers, I frown or leer; if he is a coward or given to contortions, I cringe, or twist my legs until I have to stop writing to undo the knot. I bow with him, eat with him, and gnaw my moustache with him. If the character be a lady with an exquisite laugh, I suddenly terrify you by laughing exquisitely. One reads of the astounding versatility of an actor who is stout and lean on the same evening, but what is he to the novelist who is a dozen persons within the hour? Morally, I fear, we must deteriorate— but this is a subject I may wisely edge away from.

We always spoke to each other in broad Scotch (I think in it still), but now and again she would use a word that was new to me, or I might hear one of her contemporaries use it. Now is my opportunity to angle for its meaning. If I ask, boldly, what was chat word she used just now, something like "bilbie" or "silvendy"? she blushes, and says she never said anything so common, or hoots! it is some auld-farrant word about which she can tell me nothing. But if in the course of conversation I remark casually, "Did he find bilbie?" or "Was that quite silvendy?" (though the sense of the question is vague to me) she falls into the trap, and the words explain themselves in her replies. Or maybe today she sees whither I am leading her, and such is her sensitiveness that she is quite hurt. The humour goes out of her face (to find bilbie in some more silvendy spot), and her reproachful eyes—but now I am on the arm of her chair, and we have made it up. Nevertheless, I shall get no more old-world Scotch out of her this forenoon, she weeds her talk determinedly, and it is as great a falling away as when the mutch gives place to the cap.

I am off for my afternoon walk, and she has promised to bar the door behind me and open it to none. When I return,—well, the door is still barred, but she is looking both furtive and elated. I should say that she is burning to tell me something, but cannot tell it without exposing herself. Has she opened the door, and if so, why? I don't ask, but I watch. It is she who is sly now.

"Have you been in the east room since you came in?" she asks, with apparent indifference.

"No; why do you ask?"

"Oh, I just thought you might have looked in."

"Is there anything new there?"

"I dinna say there is, but—but just go and see."

"There can't be anything new if you kept the door barred," I say cleverly.

This crushes her for a moment; but her eagerness that I should see is greater than her fear. I set off for the east room, and she follows, affecting humility, but with triumph in her eye. How often those little scenes took place! I was never told of the new purchase, I was lured into its presence, and then she waited timidly for my start of surprise.

"Do you see it?" she says anxiously, and I see it, and hear it, for this time it is a bran-new wicker chair, of the kind that whisper to themselves for the first six months.

"A going-about body was selling them in a cart," my mother begins, and what followed presents itself to my eyes before she can utter another word. Ten minutes at the least did she stand at the door argy-bargying with that man. But it would be cruelty to scold a woman so uplifted.

"Fifteen shillings he wanted," she cries, "but what do you think I beat him down to?"

"Seven and sixpence?"

She claps her hands with delight. "Four shillings, as I'm a living woman!" she crows: never was a woman fonder of a bargain.

I gaze at the purchase with the amazement expected of me, and the chair itself crinkles and shudders to hear what it went for (or is it merely chuckling at her?). "And the man said it cost himself five shillings," my mother continues exultantly. You would have thought her the hardest person had not a knock on the wall summoned us about this time to my sister's side. Though in bed she has been listening, and this is what she has to say, in a voice that makes my mother very indignant, "You drive a bargain! I'm thinking ten shillings was nearer what you paid."

"Four shillings to a penny!" says my mother.

"I daresay," says my sister; "but after you paid him the money I heard you in the little bedroom press. What were you doing there?"

My mother winces. "I may have given him a present of an old topcoat," she falters. "He looked ill-happit. But that was after I made the bargain."

"Were there bairns in the cart?"

"There might have been a bit lassie in the cart."

"I thought as much. What did you give her? I heard you in the pantry."

"Four shillings was what I got that chair for," replies my mother firmly. If I don't interfere there will be a coldness between them for at least a minute. "There is blood on your finger," I say to my mother.

"So there is," she says, concealing her hand.

"Blood!" exclaims my sister anxiously, and then with a cry of triumph, "I warrant it's jelly. You gave that lassie one of the jelly cans!"

The Glasgow waiter brings up tea, and presently my sister is able to rise, and after a sharp fight I am expelled from the kitchen. The last thing I do as maid of all work is to lug upstairs the clothes-basket which has just arrived with the mangling. Now there is delicious linen for my mother to finger; there was always rapture on her face when the clothes-basket came in; it never failed to make her once more the active genius of the house. I may leave her now with her sheets and collars and napkins and fronts. Indeed, she probably orders me to go. A son is all very well, but suppose he were to tread on that counterpane!

My sister is but and I am ben—I mean she is in the east end and I am in the west—tuts, tuts! let us get at the English of this by striving: she is in the kitchen and I am at my desk in the parlour. I hope I may not be disturbed, for tonight I must make my hero say "Darling," and it needs both privacy and concentration. In a word, let me admit (though I should like to beat about the bush) that I have sat down to a love-chapter. Too long has it been avoided, Albert has called Marion "dear" only as yet (between you and me these are not their real names), but though the public will probably read the word without blinking, it went off in my hands with a bang. They tell me—the Sassenach tell me—that in time I shall be able without a blush to make Albert say "darling," and even gather her up in his arms, but I begin to doubt it; the moment sees me as shy as ever; I still find it advisable to lock the door, and then—no witness save the dog—I "do" it dourly with my teeth clenched, while the dog retreats into the far corner and moans. The bolder Englishman (I am told) will write a love-chapter and then go out, quite coolly, to dinner, but such goings on are contrary to the Scotch nature; even the great novelists dared not. Conceive Mr. Stevenson left alone with a hero, a heroine, and a proposal impending (he does not know where to look). Sir Walter in the same circumstances gets out of the room by making his love-scenes take place between the end of one chapter and the beginning of the next, but he could afford to do anything, and the small fry must e'en to their task, moan the dog as he may. So I have yoked to mine when, enter my mother, looking wistful.

"I suppose you are terrible thrang," she says.

"Well, I am rather busy, but—what is it you want me to do?"

"It would be a shame to ask you."

"Still, ask me."

"I am so terrified they may be filed."

"You want me to—?"

"If you would just come up, and help me to fold the sheets!"

The sheets are folded and I return to Albert. I lock the door, and at last I am bringing my hero forward nicely (my knee in the small of his back), when this startling question is shot by my sister through the key-hole—

"Where did you put the carrot-grater?"

It will all have to be done over again if I let Albert go for a moment, so, gripping him hard, I shout indignantly that I have not seen the carrot-grater.

"Then what did you grate the carrots on?" asks the voice, and the door-handle is shaken just as I shake Albert.

"On a broken cup," I reply with surprising readiness, and I get to work again but am less engrossed, for a conviction grows on me that I put the carrot-grater in the drawer of the sewing-machine.

I am wondering whether I should confess or brazen it out, when I hear my sister going hurriedly upstairs. I have a presentiment that she has gone to talk about me, and I basely open my door and listen.

"Just look at that, mother!"

"Is it a dish-cloth?"

"That's what it is now."

"Losh behears! it's one of the new table-napkins."

"That's what it was. He has been polishing the kitchen grate with it!" (I remember!)

"Woe's me! That is what comes of his not letting me budge from this room. O, it is a watery Sabbath when men take to doing women's work!"

"It defies the face of clay, mother, to fathom what makes him so senseless."

"Oh, it's that weary writing."

"And the worst of it is he will talk tomorrow as if he had done wonders."

"That's the way with the whole clanjam-fray of them."

"Yes, but as usual you will humour him, mother."

"Oh, well, it pleases him, you see," says my mother, "and we can have our laugh when his door's shut."

"He is most terribly handless."

"He is all that, but, poor soul, he does his best."

VII

R. L. S.

These familiar initials are, I suppose, the best beloved in recent literature, certainly they are the sweetest to me, but there was a time when my mother could not abide them. She said "That Stevenson man" with a sneer, and, it was never easy to her to sneer. At thought of him her face would become almost hard, which seems incredible, and she would knit her lips and fold her arms, and reply with a stiff "oh" if you mentioned his aggravating name. In the novels we have a way of writing of our heroine, "she drew herself up haughtily," and when mine draw themselves up haughtily I see my mother thinking of Robert Louis Stevenson. He knew her opinion of him, and would write, "My ears tingled yesterday; I sair doubt she has been miscalling me again." But the more she miscalled him the more he delighted in her, and she was informed of this, and at once said, "The scoundrel!" If you would know what was his unpardonable crime, it was this: he wrote better books than mine.

I remember the day she found it out, which was not, however, the day she admitted it. That day, when I should have been at my work, she came upon me in the kitchen, "The Master of Ballantrae" beside me, but I was not reading: my head lay heavy on the table, and to her anxious eyes, I doubt not, I was the picture of woe. "Not writing!" I echoed, no, I was not writing, I saw no use in ever trying to write again. And down, I suppose, went my head once more. She misunderstood, and thought the blow had fallen; I had awakened to the discovery, always dreaded by her, that I had written myself dry; I was no better than an empty ink-bottle. She wrung her hands, but indignation came to her with my explanation, which was that while R. L. S. was at it we others were only 'prentices cutting our fingers on his tools. "I could never thole his books," said my mother immediately, and indeed vindictively.

"You have not read any of them," I reminded her.

"And never will," said she with spirit.

And I have no doubt that she called him a dark character that very day. For weeks too, if not for months, she adhered to her determination not to read him, though I, having come to my senses and seen that there is a place for the 'prentice, was taking a pleasure, almost malicious, in putting "The Master of Ballantrae" in her way. I would place it on her table so that it said good-morning to her when she rose. She would frown, and carrying it downstairs, as if she had it in the tongs, replace it on its book-shelf. I would wrap it up in the cover she had made for the latest Carlyle: she would skin it contemptuously and again bring it down. I would hide her spectacles in it, and lay it on top of the clothes-basket and prop it up invitingly open against her tea-pot. And at last I got her, though I forget by which of many contrivances. What I recall vividly is a key-hole view, to which another member of the family invited me. Then I saw my mother wrapped up in "The Master of Ballantrae" and muttering the music to herself, nodding her head in approval, and taking a stealthy glance at the foot of each page before she began at the top. Nevertheless she had an ear for the door, for when I bounced in she had been too clever for me; there was no book to be seen, only an apron on her lap and she was gazing out at the window. Some such conversation as this followed:—

"You have been sitting very quietly, mother."

"I always sit quietly, I never do anything, I'm just a finished stocking."

"Have you been reading?"

"Do I ever read at this time of day?"

"What is that in your lap?"

"Just my apron."

"Is that a book beneath the apron?"

"It might be a book."

"Let me see."

"Go away with you to your work."

But I lifted the apron. "Why, it's 'The Master of Ballantrae!'" I exclaimed, shocked.

"So it is!" said my mother, equally surprised. But I looked sternly at her, and perhaps she blushed.

"Well what do you think: not nearly equal to mine?" said I with humour.

"Nothing like them," she said determinedly.

"Not a bit," said I, though whether with a smile or a groan is immaterial; they would have meant the same thing. Should I put the book back on its shelf? I asked, and she replied that I could put it wherever I liked for all she cared, so long as I took it out of her sight (the implication was that it had stolen on to her lap while she was looking out at the window). My behaviour may seem small, but I gave her a last chance, for I said that some people found it a book there was no putting down until they reached the last page.

"I'm no that kind," replied my mother.

Nevertheless our old game with the haver of a thing, as she called it, was continued, with this difference, that it was now she who carried the book covertly upstairs, and I who replaced it on the shelf, and several times we caught each other in the act, but not a word said either of us; we were grown self-conscious. Much of the play no doubt I forget, but one incident I remember clearly. She had come down to sit beside me while I wrote, and sometimes, when I looked up, her eye was not on me, but on the shelf where "The Master of Ballantrae" stood inviting her. Mr. Stevenson's books are not for the shelf, they are for the hand; even when you lay them down, let it be on the table for the next comer. Being the most sociable that man has penned in our time, they feel very lonely up there in a stately row. I think their eye is on you the moment you enter the room, and so you are drawn to look at them, and you take a volume down with the impulse that induces one to unchain the dog. And the result is not dissimilar, for in another moment you two are at play. Is there any other modern writer who gets round you in this way? Well, he had given my mother the look which in the ball-room means, "Ask me for this waltz," and she ettled to do it, but felt that her more dutiful course was to sit out the dance with this other less entertaining partner. I wrote on doggedly, but could hear the whispering.

"Am I to be a wall-flower?" asked James Durie reproachfully. (It must have been leap-year.)

"Speak lower," replied my mother, with an uneasy look at me.

"Pooh!" said James contemptuously, "that kail-runtle!"

"I winna have him miscalled," said my mother, frowning.

"I am done with him," said James (wiping his cane with his cambric handkerchief), and his sword clattered deliciously (I cannot think this was accidental), which made my mother sigh. Like the man he was, he followed up his advantage with a comparison that made me dip viciously.

"A prettier sound that," said he, clanking his sword again, "than the clack-clack of your young friend's shuttle."

"Whist!" cried my mother, who had seen me dip.

"Then give me your arm," said James, lowering his voice.

"I dare not," answered my mother. "He's so touchy about you."

"Come, come," he pressed her, "you are certain to do it sooner or later, so why not now?"

"Wait till he has gone for his walk," said my mother; "and, forbye that, I'm ower old to dance with you."

"How old are you?" he inquired.

"You're gey an' pert!" cried my mother.

"Are you seventy?"

"Off and on," she admitted.

"Pooh," he said, "a mere girl!"

She replied instantly, "I'm no' to be catched with chaff"; but she smiled and rose as if he had stretched out his hand and got her by the finger-tip.

After that they whispered so low (which they could do as they were now much nearer each other) that I could catch only one remark. It came from James, and seems to show the tenor of their whisperings, for his words were, "Easily enough, if you slip me beneath your shawl."

That is what she did, and furthermore she left the room guiltily, muttering something about redding up the drawers. I suppose I smiled wanly to myself, or conscience must have been nibbling at my mother, for in less than five minutes she was back, carrying her accomplice openly, and she thrust him with positive viciousness into the place where my Stevenson had lost a tooth (as the writer whom he most resembled would have said). And then like a good mother she took up one of her son's books and read it most determinedly. It had become a touching incident to me, and I remember how we there and then agreed upon a compromise she was to read the enticing thing just to convince herself of its inferiority.

"The Master of Ballantrae" is not the best. Conceive the glory, which was my mother's, of knowing from a trustworthy source that there are at least three better awaiting you on the same shelf. She did not know Alan Breck yet, and he was as anxious to step down as Mr. Bally himself. John Silver was there, getting into his leg, so that she should not have to wait a moment, and roaring, "I'll lay to that!" when she told me consolingly that she could not thole pirate stories. Not to know these gentlemen, what is it like? It is like never having been in love. But they are in the house! That is like knowing that you will fall in love tomorrow morning. With one word, by drawing one mournful face, I could have got my mother to abjure the jam-shelf—nay, I might have managed it by merely saying that she had enjoyed "The Master of Ballantrae." For you must remember that she only read it to persuade herself (and me) of its unworthiness, and that the reason she wanted to read the others was to get further proof. All this she made plain to me, eyeing me a little anxiously the while, and of course I accepted the explanation. Alan is the biggest child of them all, and I doubt not that she thought so, but curiously enough her views of him are among the things I have forgotten. But how enamoured she was of "Treasure Island," and how faithful she tried to be to me all the time she was reading it! I had to put my hands over her eyes to let her know that I had entered the room, and even then she might try to read between my fingers, coming to herself presently, however, to say "It's a haver of a book."

"Those pirate stories are so uninteresting," I would reply without fear, for she was too engrossed to see through me. "Do you think you will finish this one?"

"I may as well go on with it since I have begun it," my mother says, so slyly that my sister and I shake our heads at each other to imply, "Was there ever such a woman!"

"There are none of those one-legged scoundrels in my books," I say.

"Better without them," she replies promptly.

"I wonder, mother, what it is about the man that so infatuates the public?"

"He takes no hold of me," she insists. "I would a hantle rather read your books."

I offer obligingly to bring one of them to her, and now she looks at me suspiciously. "You surely believe I like yours best," she says with instant anxiety, and I soothe her by assurances, and retire advising her to read on, just to see if she can find out how he misleads the public. "Oh, I may take a look at it again by-and-by," she says indifferently, but nevertheless the probability is that as the door shuts the book opens, as if by some mechanical contrivance. I remember how she read "Treasure Island," holding it close to the ribs of the fire (because she could not spare a moment to rise and light the gas), and how, when bed-time came, and we coaxed, remonstrated, scolded, she said quite fiercely, clinging to the book, "I dinna lay my head on a pillow this night till I see how that laddie got out of the barrel."

After this, I think, he was as bewitching as the laddie in the barrel to her—Was he not always a laddie in the barrel himself, climbing in for apples while we all stood around, like gamins, waiting for a bite? He was the spirit of boyhood tugging at the skirts of this old world of ours and compelling it to come back and play. And I suppose my mother felt this, as so many have felt it: like others she was a little scared at first to find herself skipping again, with this masterful child at the rope, but soon she gave him her hand and set off with him for the meadow, not an apology between the two of them for the author left behind. But near to the end did she admit (in words) that he had a way with him which was beyond her son. "Silk and sacking, that is what we are," she was informed, to which she would reply obstinately, "Well, then, I prefer sacking."

"But if he had been your son?"

"But he is not."

"You wish he were?"

"I dinna deny but what I could have found room for him."

And still at times she would smear him with the name of black (to his delight when he learned the reason). That was when some podgy red-sealed blue-crossed letter arrived from Vailima, inviting me to journey thither. (His directions were, "You take the boat at San Francisco, and then my place is the second to the left.") Even London seemed to her to carry me so far away that I often took a week to the journey (the first six days in getting her used to the idea), and these letters terrified her. It was not the finger of Jim Hawkins she now saw beckoning me across the seas, it was John Silver, waving a crutch. Seldom, I believe, did I read straight through one of these Vailima letters; when in the middle I suddenly remembered who was upstairs and what she was probably doing, and I ran to her, three steps at a jump, to find her, lips pursed, hands folded, a picture of gloom.

"I have a letter from—"

"So I have heard."

"Would you like to hear it?"

"No."

"Can you not abide him?"

"I cauna thole him."

"Is he a black?"

"He is all that."

Well, Vailima was the one spot on earth I had any great craving to visit, but I think she always knew I would never leave her. Sometime, she said, she should like me to go, but not until she was laid away. "And how small I have grown this last winter. Look at my wrists. It canna be long now." No, I never thought of going, was never absent for a day from her without reluctance, and never walked so quickly as when I was going back. In the meantime that happened which put an end forever to my scheme of travel. I shall never go up the Road of Loving Hearts now, on "a wonderful clear night of stars," to meet the man coming toward me on a horse. It is still a wonderful clear night of stars, but the road is empty. So I never saw the dear king of us all. But before he had written books he was in my part of the country with a fishing-wand in his hand, and I like to think that I was the boy who met him that day by Queen Margaret's burn, where the rowans are, and busked a fly for him, and stood watching, while his lithe figure rose and fell as he cast and hinted back from the crystal waters of Noran-side.

VIII

A Panic in the House

I was sitting at my desk in London when a telegram came announcing that my mother was again dangerously ill, and I seized my hat and hurried to the station. It is not a memory of one night only. A score of times, I am sure, I was called north thus suddenly, and reached our little town trembling, head out at railway-carriage window for a glance at a known face which would answer the question on mine. These illnesses came as regularly as the backend of the year, but were less regular in going, and through them all, by night and by day, I see my sister moving so unwearyingly, so lovingly, though with failing strength, that I bow my head in reverence for her. She was wearing herself done. The doctor advised us to engage a nurse, but the mere word frightened my mother, and we got between her and the door as if the woman was already on the stair. To have a strange woman in my mother's room—you who are used to them cannot conceive what it meant to us.

Then we must have a servant. This seemed only less horrible. My father turned up his sleeves and clutched the besom. I tossed aside my papers, and was ready to run the errands. He answered the door, I kept the fires going, he gave me a lesson in cooking, I showed him how to make beds, one of us wore an apron. It was not for long. I was led to my desk, the newspaper was put into my father's hand. "But a servant!" we cried, and would have fallen to again. "No servant, comes into this house," said my sister quite fiercely, and, oh, but my mother was relieved to hear her! There were many such scenes, a year of them, I daresay, before we yielded.

I cannot say which of us felt it most. In London I was used to servants, and in moments of irritation would ring for them furiously, though doubtless my manner changed as they opened the door. I have even held my own with gentlemen in plush, giving one my hat, another my stick, and a third my coat, and all done with little more trouble than I should have expended in putting the three articles on the chair myself. But this bold deed, and other big things of the kind, I did that I might tell my mother of them afterwards, while I sat on the end of her bed, and her face beamed with astonishment and mirth.

From my earliest days I had seen servants. The manse had a servant, the bank had another; one of their uses was to pounce upon, and carry away in stately manner, certain naughty boys who played with me. The banker did not seem really great to me, but his servant—oh yes. Her boots cheeped all the way down the church aisle; it was common report that she had flesh everyday for her dinner; instead of meeting her lover at the pump she walked him into the country, and he returned with wild roses in his buttonhole, his hand up to hide them, and on his face the troubled look of those who know that if they take this lady they must give up drinking from the saucer for evermore. For the lovers were really common men, until she gave them that glance over the shoulder which, I have noticed, is the fatal gift of servants.

According to legend we once had a servant—in my childhood I could show the mark of it on my forehead, and even point her out to other boys, though she was now merely a wife with a house of her own. But even while I boasted I doubted. Reduced to life-size she may have been but a woman who came in to help. I shall say no more about her, lest someone comes forward to prove that she went home at night.

Never shall I forget my first servant. I was eight or nine, in velveteen, diamond socks ("Cross your legs when they look at you," my mother had said, "and put your thumb in your pocket and leave the top of your handkerchief showing"), and I had travelled by rail to visit a relative. He had a servant, and as I was to be his guest she must be my servant also for the time being—you may be sure I had got my mother to put this plainly before me ere I set off. My relative met me at the station, but I wasted no time in hoping I found him well. I did not even cross my legs for him, so eager was I to hear whether she was still there. A sister greeted me at the door, but I chafed at having to be kissed; at once I made for the kitchen, where, I knew, they reside, and there she was, and I crossed my legs and put one thumb in my pocket, and the handkerchief was showing. Afterwards I stopped strangers on the highway with an offer to show her to them through the kitchen window, and I doubt not the first letter I ever wrote told my mother what they are like when they are so near that you can put your fingers into them.

But now when we could have servants for ourselves I shrank from the thought. It would not be the same house; we should have to dissemble; I saw myself speaking English the long day through. You only know the shell of a Scot until you have entered his home circle; in his office, in clubs, at social gatherings where you and he seem to be getting on so well he is really a house with all the shutters closed and the door locked. He is not opaque of set purpose, often it is against his will—it is certainly against mine, I try to keep my shutters open and my foot in the door but they will bang to. In many ways my mother was as reticent as myself, though her manners were as gracious as mine were rough (in vain, alas! all the honest oiling of them), and my sister was the most reserved of us all; you might at times see a light through one of my chinks: she was double-shuttered. Now, it seems to be a law of nature that we must show our true selves at sometime, and as the Scot must do it at home, and squeeze a day into an hour, what follows is that there he is self-revealing in the superlative degree, the feelings so long dammed up overflow, and thus a Scotch family are probably better acquainted with each other, and more ignorant of the life outside their circle, than any other family in the world. And as knowledge is sympathy, the affection existing between them is almost painful in its intensity; they have not more to give than their neighbours, but it is bestowed upon a few instead of being distributed among many; they are reputed niggardly, but for family affection at least they pay in gold. In this, I believe, we shall find the true explanation why Scotch literature, since long before the days of Burns, has been so often inspired by the domestic hearth, and has treated it with a passionate understanding.

Must a woman come into our house and discover that I was not such a dreary dog as I had the reputation of being? Was I to be seen at last with the veil of dourness lifted? My company voice is so low and unimpressive that my first remark is merely an intimation that I am about to speak (like the whir of the clock before it strikes): must it be revealed that I had another voice, that there was one door I never opened without leaving my reserve on the mat? Ah, that room, must its secrets be disclosed? So joyous they were when my mother was well, no wonder we were merry. Again and again she had been given back to us; it was for the glorious today we thanked God; in our hearts we knew and in our prayers confessed that the fill of delight had been given us, whatever might befall. We had not to wait till all was over to know its value; my mother used to say, "We never understand how little we need in this world until we know the loss of it," and there can be few truer sayings, but during her last years we exulted daily in the possession of her as much as we can exult in her memory. No wonder, I say, that we were merry, but we liked to show it to God alone, and to Him only our agony during those many night-alarms, when lights flickered in the house and white faces were round my mother's bedside. Not for other eyes those long vigils when, night about, we sat watching, nor the awful nights when we stood together, teeth clenched—waiting—it must be now. And it was not then; her hand became cooler, her breathing more easy; she smiled to us. Once more I could work by snatches, and was glad, but what was the result to me compared to the joy of hearing that voice from the other room? There lay all the work I was ever proud of, the rest is but honest craftsmanship done to give her coal and food and softer pillows. My thousand letters that she so carefully preserved, always sleeping with the last beneath the sheet, where one was found when she died—they are the only writing of mine of which I shall ever boast. I would not there had been one less though I could have written an immortal book for it.

How my sister toiled—to prevent a stranger's getting any footing in the house! And how, with the same object, my mother strove to "do for herself" once more. She pretended that she was always well now, and concealed her ailments so craftily that we had to probe for them:—

"I think you are not feeling well today?"

"I am perfectly well."

"Where is the pain?"

"I have no pain to speak of."

"Is it at your heart?"

"No."

"Is your breathing hurting you?"

"Not it."

"Do you feel those stounds in your head again?"

"No, no, I tell you there is nothing the matter with me."

"Have you a pain in your side?"

"Really, it's most provoking I canna put my hand to my side without your thinking I have a pain there."

"You have a pain in your side!"

"I might have a pain in my side."

"And you were trying to hide it! Is it very painful?"

"It's—it's no so bad but what I can bear it."

Which of these two gave in first I cannot tell, though to me fell the duty of persuading them, for whichever she was she rebelled as soon as the other showed signs of yielding, so that sometimes I had two converts in the week but never both on the same day. I would take them separately, and press the one to yield for the sake of the other, but they saw so easily through my artifice. My mother might go bravely to my sister and say, "I have been thinking it over, and I believe I would like a servant fine—once we got used to her."

"Did he tell you to say that?" asks my sister sharply.

"I say it of my own free will."

"He put you up to it, I am sure, and he told you not to let on that you did it to lighten my work."

"Maybe he did, but I think we should get one."

"Not for my sake," says my sister obstinately, and then my mother comes ben to me to say delightedly, "She winna listen to reason!"

But at last a servant was engaged; we might be said to be at the window, gloomily waiting for her now, and it was with such words as these that we sought to comfort each other and ourselves:—

"She will go early to her bed."

"She needna often be seen upstairs."

"We'll set her to the walking everyday."

"There will be a many errands for her to run. We'll tell her to take her time over them."

"Three times she shall go to the kirk every Sabbath, and we'll egg her on to attending the lectures in the hall."

"She is sure to have friends in the town. We'll let her visit them often."

"If she dares to come into your room, mother!"

"Mind this, everyone of you, servant or no servant, I fold all the linen mysel."

"She shall not get cleaning out the east room."

"Nor putting my chest of drawers in order."

"Nor tidying up my manuscripts."

"I hope she's a reader, though. You could set her down with a book, and then close the door canny on her."

And so on. Was ever servant awaited so apprehensively? And then she came—at an anxious time, too, when her worth could be put to the proof at once—and from first to last she was a treasure. I know not what we should have done without her.

IX

My Heroine

When it was known that I had begun another story my mother might ask what it was to be about this time.

"Fine we can guess who it is about," my sister would say pointedly.

"Maybe you can guess, but it is beyond me," says my mother, with the meekness of one who knows that she is a dull person.

My sister scorned her at such times. "What woman is in all his books?" she would demand.

"I'm sure I canna say," replies my mother determinedly. "I thought the women were different everytime."

"Mother, I wonder you can be so audacious! Fine you know what woman I mean."

"How can I know? What woman is it? You should bear in mind that I hinna your cleverness" (they were constantly giving each other little knocks).

"I won't give you the satisfaction of saying her name. But this I will say, it is high time he was keeping her out of his books."

And then as usual my mother would give herself away unconsciously. "That is what I tell him," she says chuckling, "and he tries to keep me out, but he canna; it's more than he can do!"

On an evening after my mother had gone to bed, the first chapter would be brought upstairs, and I read, sitting at the foot of the bed, while my sister watched to make my mother behave herself, and my father cried H'sh! when there were interruptions. All would go well at the start, the reflections were accepted with a little nod of the head, the descriptions of scenery as ruts on the road that must be got over at a walking pace (my mother did not care for scenery, and that is why there is so little of it in my books). But now I am reading too quickly, a little apprehensively, because I know that the next paragraph begins with—let us say with, "Along this path came a woman": I had intended to rush on here in a loud bullying voice, but "Along this path came a woman" I read, and stop. Did I hear a faint sound from the other end of the bed? Perhaps I did not; I may only have been listening for it, but I falter and look up. My sister and I look sternly at my mother. She bites her under-lip and clutches the bed with both hands, really she is doing her best for me, but first comes a smothered gurgling sound, then her hold on herself relaxes and she shakes with mirth.

"That's a way to behave!" cries my sister.

"I cannot help it," my mother gasps.

"And there's nothing to laugh at."

"It's that woman," my mother explains unnecessarily.

"Maybe she's not the woman you think her," I say, crushed.

"Maybe not," says my mother doubtfully. "What was her name?"

"Her name," I answer with triumph, "was not Margaret"; but this makes her ripple again. "I have so many names nowadays," she mutters.

"H'sh!" says my father, and the reading is resumed.

Perhaps the woman who came along the path was of tall and majestic figure, which should have shown my mother that I had contrived to start my train without her this time. But it did not.

"What are you laughing at now?" says my sister severely. "Do you not hear that she was a tall, majestic woman?"

"It's the first time I ever heard it said of her," replies my mother.

"But she is."

"Ke fy, havers!"

"The book says it."

"There will be a many queer things in the book. What was she wearing?"

I have not described her clothes. "That's a mistake," says my mother. "When I come upon a woman in a book, the first thing I want to know about her is whether she was good-looking, and the second, how she was put on."

The woman on the path was eighteen years of age, and of remarkable beauty.

"That settles you," says my sister.

"I was no beauty at eighteen," my mother admits, but here my father interferes unexpectedly. "There wasna your like in this countryside at eighteen," says he stoutly.

"Pooh!" says she, well pleased.

"Were you plain, then?" we ask.

"Sal," she replies briskly, "I was far from plain."

"H'sh!"

Perhaps in the next chapter this lady (or another) appears in a carriage.

"I assure you we're mounting in the world," I hear my mother murmur, but I hurry on without looking up. The lady lives in a house where there are footmen—but the footmen have come on the scene too hurriedly. "This is more than I can stand," gasps my mother, and just as she is getting the better of a fit of laughter, "Footman, give me a drink of water," she cries, and this sets her off again. Often the readings had to end abruptly because her mirth brought on violent fits of coughing.

Sometimes I read to my sister alone, and she assured me that she could not see my mother among the women this time. This she said to humour me. Presently she would slip upstairs to announce triumphantly, "You are in again!"

Or in the small hours I might make a confidant of my father, and when I had finished reading he would say thoughtfully, "That lassie is very natural. Some of the ways you say she had—your mother had them just the same. Did you ever notice what an extraordinary woman your mother is?"

Then would I seek my mother for comfort. She was the more ready to give it because of her profound conviction that if I was found out— that is, if readers discovered how frequently and in how many guises she appeared in my books—the affair would become a public scandal.

"You see Jess is not really you," I begin inquiringly.

"Oh no, she is another kind of woman altogether," my mother says, and then spoils the compliment by adding naïvely, "She had but two rooms and I have six."

I sigh. "Without counting the pantry, and it's a great big pantry," she mutters.

This was not the sort of difference I could greatly plume myself upon, and honesty would force me to say, "As far as that goes, there was a time when you had but two rooms yourself—"

"That's long since," she breaks in. "I began with an up-the-stair, but I always had it in my mind—I never mentioned it, but there it was—to have the down-the-stair as well. Ay, and I've had it this many a year."

"Still, there is no denying that Jess had the same ambition."

"She had, but to her two-roomed house she had to stick all her born days. Was that like me?"

"No, but she wanted—"

"She wanted, and I wanted, but I got and she didna. That's the difference betwixt her and me."

"If that is all the difference, it is little credit I can claim for having created her."

My mother sees that I need soothing. "That is far from being all the difference," she would say eagerly. "There's my silk, for instance. Though I say it mysel, there's not a better silk in the valley of Strathmore. Had Jess a silk of any kind—not to speak of a silk like that?"

"Well, she had no silk, but you remember how she got that cloak with beads."

"An eleven and a bit! Hoots, what was that to boast of! I tell you, every single yard of my silk cost—"

"Mother, that is the very way Jess spoke about her cloak!"

She lets this pass, perhaps without hearing it, for solicitude about her silk has hurried her to the wardrobe where it hangs.

"Ah, mother, I am afraid that was very like Jess!"

"How could it be like her when she didna even have a wardrobe? I tell you what, if there had been a real Jess and she had boasted to me about her cloak with beads, I would have said to her in a careless sort of voice, 'Step across with me, Jess and I'll let you see something that is hanging in my wardrobe.' That would have lowered her pride!"

"I don't believe that is what you would have done, mother."

Then a sweeter expression would come into her face. "No," she would say reflectively, "it's not."

"What would you have done? I think I know."

"You canna know. But I'm thinking I would have called to mind that she was a poor woman, and ailing, and terrible windy about her cloak, and I would just have said it was a beauty and that I wished I had one like it."

"Yes, I am certain that is what you would have done. But oh, mother, that is just how Jess would have acted if some poorer woman than she had shown her a new shawl."

"Maybe, but though I hadna boasted about my silk I would have wanted to do it."

"Just as Jess would have been fidgeting to show off her eleven and a bit!"

It seems advisable to jump to another book; not to my first, because—well, as it was my first there would naturally be something of my mother in it, and not to the second, as it was my first novel and not much esteemed even in our family. (But the little touches of my mother in it are not so bad.) Let us try the story about the minister.

My mother's first remark is decidedly damping. "Many a time in my young days," she says, "I played about the Auld Licht manse, but I little thought I should live to be the mistress of it!"

"But Margaret is not you."

"N-no, oh no. She had a very different life from mine. I never let on to a soul that she is me!"

"She was not meant to be you when I began. Mother, what a way you have of coming creeping in!"

"You should keep better watch on yourself."

"Perhaps if I had called Margaret by some other name—"

"I should have seen through her just the same. As soon as I heard she was the mother I began to laugh. In some ways, though, she's no' so very like me. She was long in finding out about Babbie. I'se uphaud I should have been quicker."

"Babbie, you see, kept close to the garden-wall."

"It's not the wall up at the manse that would have hidden her from me."

"She came out in the dark."

"I'm thinking she would have found me looking for her with a candle."

"And Gavin was secretive."

"That would have put me on my mettle."

"She never suspected anything."

"I wonder at her."

But my new heroine is to be a child. What has madam to say to that?

A child! Yes, she has something to say even to that. "This beats all!" are the words.

"Come, come, mother, I see what you are thinking, but I assure you that this time—"

"Of course not," she says soothingly, "oh no, she canna be me"; but anon her real thoughts are revealed by the artless remark, "I doubt, though, this is a tough job you have on hand—it is so long since I was a bairn."

We came very close to each other in those talks. "It is a queer thing," she would say softly, "that near everything you write is about this bit place. You little expected that when you began. I mind well the time when it never entered your head, anymore than mine, that you could write a page about our squares and wynds. I wonder how it has come about?"

There was a time when I could not have answered that question, but that time had long passed. "I suppose, mother, it was because you were most at home in your own town, and there was never much pleasure to me in writing of people who could not have known you, nor of squares and wynds you never passed through, nor of a country-side where you never carried your father's dinner in a flagon. There is scarce a house in all my books where I have not seemed to see you a thousand times, bending over the fireplace or winding up the clock."

"And yet you used to be in such a quandary because you knew nobody you could make your women-folk out of! Do you mind that, and how we both laughed at the notion of your having to make them out of me?"

"I remember."

"And now you've gone back to my father's time. It's more than sixty years since I carried his dinner in a flagon through the long parks of Kinnordy."

"I often go into the long parks, mother, and sit on the stile at the edge of the wood till I fancy I see a little girl coming toward me with a flagon in her hand."

"Jumping the burn (I was once so proud of my jumps!) and swinging the flagon round so quick that what was inside hadna time to fall out. I used to wear a magenta frock and a white pinafore. Did I ever tell you that?"

"Mother, the little girl in my story wears a magenta frock and a white pinafore."

"You minded that! But I'm thinking it wasna a lassie in a pinafore you saw in the long parks of Kinnordy, it was just a gey done auld woman."

"It was a lassie in a pinafore, mother, when she was far away, but when she came near it was a gey done auld woman."

"And a fell ugly one!"

"The most beautiful one I shall ever see."

"I wonder to hear you say it. Look at my wrinkled auld face."

"It is the sweetest face in all the world."

"See how the rings drop off my poor wasted finger."

"There will always be someone nigh, mother, to put them on again."

"Ay, will there! Well I know it. Do you mind how when you were but a bairn you used to say, 'Wait till I'm a man, and you'll never have a reason for greeting again?'"

I remembered.

"You used to come running into the house to say, 'There's a proud dame going down the Marywellbrae in a cloak that is black on one side and white on the other; wait till I'm a man, and you'll have one the very same.' And when I lay on gey hard beds you said, 'When I'm a man you'll lie on feathers.' You saw nothing bonny, you never heard of my setting my heart on anything, but what you flung up your head and cried, 'Wait till I'm a man.' You fair shamed me before the neighbours, and yet I was windy, too. And now it has all come true like a dream. I can call to mind not one little thing I ettled for in my lusty days that hasna been put into my hands in my auld age; I sit here useless, surrounded by the gratification of all my wishes and all my ambitions, and at times I'm near terrified, for it's as if God had mista'en me for some other woman."

"Your hopes and ambitions were so simple," I would say, but she did not like that. "They werena that simple," she would answer, flushing.

I am reluctant to leave those happy days, but the end must be faced, and as I write I seem to see my mother growing smaller and her face more wistful, and still she lingers with us, as if God had said, "Child of mine, your time has come, be not afraid." And she was not afraid, but still she lingered, and He waited, smiling. I never read any of that last book to her; when it was finished she was too heavy with years to follow a story. To me this was as if my book must go out cold into the world (like all that may come after it from me), and my sister, who took more thought for others and less for herself than any other human being I have known, saw this, and by some means unfathomable to a man coaxed my mother into being once again the woman she had been. On a day but three weeks before she died my father and I were called softly upstairs. My mother was sitting bolt upright, as she loved to sit, in her old chair by the window, with a manuscript in her hands. But she was looking about her without much understanding. "Just to please him," my sister whispered, and then in a low, trembling voice my mother began to read. I looked at my sister. Tears of woe were stealing down her face. Soon the reading became very slow and stopped. After a pause, "There was something you were to say to him," my sister reminded her. "Luck," muttered a voice as from the dead, "luck." And then the old smile came running to her face like a lamp-lighter, and she said to me, "I am ower far gone to read, but I'm thinking I am in it again!" My father put her Testament in her hands, and it fell open—as it always does—at the Fourteenth of John. She made an effort to read but could not. Suddenly she stooped and kissed the broad page. "Will that do instead?" she asked.

X

Art Thou Afraid His Power Shall Fail?

For years I had been trying to prepare myself for my mother's death, trying to foresee how she would die, seeing myself when she was dead. Even then I knew it was a vain thing I did, but I am sure there was no morbidness in it. I hoped I should be with her at the end, not as the one she looked at last but as him from whom she would turn only to look upon her best-beloved, not my arm but my sister's should be round her when she died, not my hand but my sister's should close her eyes. I knew that I might reach her too late; I saw myself open a door where there was none to greet me, and go up the old stair into the old room. But what I did not foresee was that which happened. I little thought it could come about that I should climb the old stair, and pass the door beyond which my mother lay dead, and enter another room first, and go on my knees there.

My mother's favourite paraphrase is one known in our house as David's because it was the last he learned to repeat. It was also the last thing she read—

> *Art thou afraid his power shall fail*
> *When comes thy evil day?*
> *And can an all-creating arm*
> *Grow weary or decay?*

I heard her voice gain strength as she read it, I saw her timid face take courage, but when came my evil day, then at the dawning, alas for me, I was afraid.

In those last weeks, though we did not know it, my sister was dying on her feet. For many years she had been giving her life, a little bit at a time, for another year, another month, latterly for another day, of her mother, and now she was worn out. "I'll never leave you, mother."— "Fine I know you'll never leave me." I thought that cry so pathetic at the time, but I was not to know its full significance until it was only the echo of a cry. Looking at these two then it was to me as if my mother had set out for the new country, and my sister held her back. But I see with a clearer vision now. It is no longer the mother but the daughter who is in front, and she cries, "Mother, you are lingering so long at the end, I have ill waiting for you."

But she knew no more than we how it was to be; if she seemed weary when we met her on the stair, she was still the brightest, the most active figure in my mother's room; she never complained, save when she had to depart on that walk which separated them for half an hour. How reluctantly she put on her bonnet, how we had to press her to it, and how often, having gone as far as the door, she came back to stand by my mother's side. Sometimes as we watched from the window, I could not but laugh, and yet with a pain at my heart, to see her hasting doggedly onward, not an eye for right or left, nothing in her head but the return. There was always my father in the house, than whom never was a more devoted husband, and often there were others, one daughter in particular, but they scarce dared tend my mother—this one snatched the cup jealously from their hands. My mother liked it best from her. We all knew this. "I like them fine, but I canna do without you." My sister, so unselfish in all other things, had an unwearying passion for parading it before us. It was the rich reward of her life.

The others spoke among themselves of what must come soon, and they had tears to help them, but this daughter would not speak of it, and her tears were ever slow to come. I knew that night and day she was trying to get ready for a world without her mother in it, but she must remain dumb; none of us was so Scotch as she, she must bear her agony alone, a tragic solitary Scotchwoman. Even my mother, who spoke so calmly to us of the coming time, could not mention it to her. These two, the one in bed, and the other bending over her, could only look long at each other, until slowly the tears came to my sister's eyes, and then my mother would turn away her wet face. And still neither said a word, each knew so well what was in the other's thoughts, so eloquently they spoke in silence, "Mother, I am loath to let you go," and "Oh my daughter, now that my time is near, I wish you werena quite so fond of me." But when the daughter had slipped away my mother would grip my hand and cry, "I leave her to you; you see how she has sown, it will depend on you how she is to reap." And I made promises, but I suppose neither of us saw that she had already reaped.

In the night my mother might waken and sit up in bed, confused by what she saw. While she slept, six decades or more had rolled back and she was again in her girlhood; suddenly recalled from it she was dizzy, as with the rush of the years. How had she come into this room? When she went to bed last night, after preparing her father's supper, there had been a dresser at the window: what had become of the salt-bucket, the meal-tub, the hams that should be hanging from the rafters? There were no rafters; it was a papered ceiling. She had often heard of open beds, but how came she to be lying in one? To fathom these things she would try to spring out of bed and be startled to find it a labour, as if she had been taken ill in the night. Hearing her move I might knock on the wall that separated us, this being a sign, prearranged between us, that I was near by, and so all was well, but sometimes the knocking seemed to belong to the past, and she would cry, "That is my father chapping at the door, I maun rise and let him in." She seemed to see him—and it was one much younger than herself that she saw—covered with snow, kicking clods of it from his boots, his hands swollen and chapped with sand and wet. Then I would hear—it was a common experience of the night—my sister soothing her lovingly, and turning up the light to show her where she was, helping her to the window to let her see that it was no night of snow, even humouring her by going downstairs, and opening the outer door, and calling into the darkness, "Is anybody there?" and if that was not sufficient, she would swaddle my mother in wraps and take her through the rooms of the house, lighting them one by one, pointing out familiar objects, and so guiding her slowly through the sixty odd years she had jumped too quickly. And perhaps the end of it was that my mother came to my bedside and said wistfully, "Am I an auld woman?"

But with daylight, even during the last week in which I saw her, she would be up and doing, for though pitifully frail she no longer suffered from any ailment. She seemed so well comparatively that I, having still the remnants of an illness to shake off, was to take a holiday in Switzerland, and then return for her, when we were all to go to the much-loved manse of her much-loved brother in the west country. So she had many preparations on her mind, and the morning was the time when she had any strength to carry them out. To leave her house had always been a month's work for her, it must be left in such perfect order, every corner visited and cleaned out, every chest probed to the bottom, the linen lifted out, examined and put back lovingly as if to make it lie more easily in her absence, shelves had to be re-papered, a strenuous week devoted to the garret. Less exhaustively, but with much of the old exultation in her house, this

　　　　　　　　　　　　　　　J.M. BARRIE

was done for the last time, and then there was the bringing out of her own clothes, and the spreading of them upon the bed and the pleased fingering of them, and the consultations about which should be left behind. Ah, beautiful dream! I clung to it every morning; I would not look when my sister shook her head at it, but long before each day was done I too knew that it could never be. It had come true many times, but never again. We two knew it, but when my mother, who must always be prepared so long beforehand, called for her trunk and band-boxes we brought them to her, and we stood silent, watching, while she packed.

The morning came when I was to go away. It had come a hundred times, when I was a boy, when I was an undergraduate, when I was a man, when she had seemed big and strong to me, when she was grown so little and it was I who put my arms round her. But always it was the same scene. I am not to write about it, of the parting and the turning back on the stair, and two people trying to smile, and the setting off again, and the cry that brought me back. Nor shall I say more of the silent figure in the background, always in the background, always near my mother. The last I saw of these two was from the gate. They were at the window which never passes from my eyes. I could not see my dear sister's face, for she was bending over my mother, pointing me out to her, and telling her to wave her hand and smile, because I liked it so. That action was an epitome of my sister's life.

I had been gone a fortnight when the telegram was put into my hands. I had got a letter from my sister, a few hours before, saying that all was well at home. The telegram said in five words that she had died suddenly the previous night. There was no mention of my mother, and I was three days' journey from home.

The news I got on reaching London was this: my mother did not understand that her daughter was dead, and they were waiting for me to tell her.

I need not have been such a coward. This is how these two died—for, after all, I was too late by twelve hours to see my mother alive.

Their last night was almost gleeful. In the old days that hour before my mother's gas was lowered had so often been the happiest that my pen steals back to it again and again as I write: it was the time when my mother lay smiling in bed and we were gathered round her like children at play, our reticence scattered on the floor or tossed in sport from hand to hand, the author become so boisterous that in the pauses they were holding him in check by force. Rather woful had been some attempts latterly to renew those evenings, when my mother might be brought to the verge of them, as if some familiar echo called her, but where she was she did not clearly know, because the past was roaring in her ears like a great sea. But this night was a last gift to my sister. The joyousness of their voices drew the others in the house upstairs, where for more than an hour my mother was the centre of a merry party and so clear of mental eye that they, who were at first cautious, abandoned themselves to the sport, and whatever they said, by way of humorous rally, she instantly capped as of old, turning their darts against themselves until in self-defence they were three to one, and the three hard pressed. How my sister must have been rejoicing. Once again she could cry, "Was there ever such a woman!" They tell me that such a happiness was on the daughter's face that my mother commented on it, that having risen to go they sat down again, fascinated by the radiance of these two. And when eventually they went, the last words they heard were, "They are gone, you see, mother, but I am here, I will never leave you," and "Na, you winna leave me; fine I know that." For sometime afterwards their voices could be heard from downstairs, but what they talked of is not known. And then came silence. Had I been at home I should have been in the room again several times, turning the handle of the door softly, releasing it so that it did not creak, and standing looking at them. It had been so a thousand times. But that night, would I have slipped out again, mind at rest, or should I have seen the change coming while they slept?

Let it be told in the fewest words. My sister awoke next morning with a headache. She had always been a martyr to headaches, but this one, like many another, seemed to be unusually severe. Nevertheless she rose and lit my mother's fire and brought up her breakfast, and then had to return to bed. She was not able to write her daily letter to me, saying how my mother was, and almost the last thing she did was to ask my father to write it, and not to let on that she was ill, as it would distress me. The doctor was called, but she rapidly became unconscious. In this state she was removed from my mother's bed to another. It was discovered that she was suffering from an internal disease. No one had guessed it. She herself never knew. Nothing could be done. In this unconsciousness she passed away, without knowing that she was leaving her mother. Had I known, when I heard of her death, that she had been saved that pain, surely I could have gone home more bravely with the words,

Art thou afraid His power fail
When comes thy evil day?

Ah, you would think so, I should have thought so, but I know myself now. When I reached London I did hear how my sister died, but still I was afraid. I saw myself in my mother's room telling her why the door of the next room was locked, and I was afraid. God had done so much, and yet I could not look confidently to Him for the little that was left to do. "O ye of little faith!" These are the words I seem to hear my mother saying to me now, and she looks at me so sorrowfully.

He did it very easily, and it has ceased to seem marvellous to me because it was so plainly His doing. My timid mother saw the one who was never to leave her carried unconscious from the room, and she did not break down. She who used to wring her hands if her daughter was gone for a moment never asked for her again, they were afraid to mention her name; an awe fell upon them. But I am sure they need not have been so anxious. There are mysteries in life and death, but this was not one of them. A child can understand what happened. God said that my sister must come first, but He put His hand on my mother's eyes at that moment and she was altered.

They told her that I was on my way home, and she said with a confident smile, "He will come as quick as trains can bring him." That is my reward, that is what I have got for my books. Everything I could do for her in this life I have done since I was a boy; I look back through the years and I cannot see the smallest thing left undone.

They were buried together on my mother's seventy-sixth birthday, though there had been three days between their deaths. On the last day, my mother insisted on rising from bed and going through the house. The arms that had so often helped her on that journey were now cold in death, but there were others only less loving, and she went slowly from room to room like one bidding good-bye, and in mine she said, "The beautiful rows upon rows of books, ant he said everyone of them was mine, all mine!" and in the east room, which was her greatest triumph, she said caressingly, "My nain bonny room!" All this time there seemed to be something that she wanted, but the one was dead who always knew what she wanted, and they produced many things at which she shook her head. They did not know then that she was dying, but they followed her through the house in some apprehension, and after she returned to bed they saw that she was becoming very weak. Once she said eagerly, "Is that you, David?" and again she thought she heard her father knocking the snow off his boots. Her desire for that which she could not name came back to her, and at last they saw that what she wanted was the old christening robe. It was brought to her, and she unfolded it with trembling, exultant hands, and when she had made sure that it was still of virgin fairness her old arms went round it adoringly, and upon her face there was the ineffable mysterious glow of motherhood. Suddenly she said, "Wha's bairn's dead? is a bairn of mine dead?" but those watching dared not speak, and then slowly as if with an effort of memory she repeated our names aloud in the order in which we were born. Only one, who should have come third among the ten, did she omit, the one in the next room, but at the end, after a pause, she said her name and repeated it again and again and again, lingering over it as if it were the most exquisite music and this her dying song. And yet it was a very commonplace name.

They knew now that she was dying. She told them to fold up the christening robe and almost sharply she watched them put it away, and then for sometime she talked of the long lovely life that had been hers, and of Him to whom she owed it. She said good-bye to them all, and at last turned her face to the side where her best-beloved had lain, and for over an hour she prayed. They only caught the words now and again, and the last they heard were "God" and "love." I think God was smiling when He took her to Him, as He had so often smiled at her during those seventy-six years.

I saw her lying dead, and her face was beautiful and serene. But it was the other room I entered first, and it was by my sister's side that I fell upon my knees. The rounded completeness of a woman's life that was my mother's had not been for her. She would not have it at the price. "I'll never leave you, mother."—"Fine I know you'll never leave me." The fierce joy of loving too much, it is a terrible thing. My sister's mouth was firmly closed, as if she had got her way.

And now I am left without them, but I trust my memory will ever go back to those happy days, not to rush through them, but dallying here and there, even as my mother wanders through my books. And if I also live to a time when age must dim my mind and the past comes sweeping back like the shades of night over the bare road of the present it will not, I believe, be my youth I shall see but hers, not a boy clinging to his mother's skirt and crying, "Wait till I'm a man, and you'll lie on feathers," but a little girl in a magenta frock and a white pinafore, who comes toward me through the long parks, singing to herself, and carrying her father's dinner in a flagon.

THE END

A Note About the Author

J.M. Barrie (1860–1937) was a Scottish novelist and playwright. Born in Kirriemuir, Barrie was raised in a strict Calvinist family. At the age of six, he lost his brother David to an ice-skating accident, a tragedy which left his family devastated and led to a strengthening in Barrie's relationship with his mother. At school, he developed a passion for reading and acting, forming a drama club with his friends in Glasgow. After graduating from the University of Edinburgh, he found work as a journalist for the *Nottingham Journal* while writing the stories that would become his first novels. *The Little White Bird* (1902), a blend of fairytale fiction and social commentary, was his first novel to feature the beloved character Peter Pan, who would take the lead in his 1904 play *Peter Pan; or the Boy Who Wouldn't Grow Up*, later adapted for a 1911 novel and immortalized in the 1953 Disney animated film. A friend of Robert Louis Stevenson, George Bernard Shaw, and H. G. Wells, Barrie is known for his relationship with the Llewelyn Davies family, whose young boys were the inspiration for his stories of Peter Pan's adventures with Wendy, Tinker Bell, and the Lost Boys on the island of Neverland.

A Note from the Publisher

Spanning many genres, from non-fiction essays to literature classics to children's books and lyric poetry, Mint Edition books showcase the master works of our time in a modern new package. The text is freshly typeset, is clean and easy to read, and features a new note about the author in each volume. Many books also include exclusive new introductory material. Every book boasts a striking new cover, which makes it as appropriate for collecting as it is for gift giving. Mint Edition books are only printed when a reader orders them, so natural resources are not wasted. We're proud that our books are never manufactured in excess and exist only in the exact quantity they need to be read and enjoyed.

bookfinity™

Discover more of your favorite classics with Bookfinity™.

- Track your reading with custom book lists.
- Get great book recommendations for your personalized Reader Type.
- Add reviews for your favorite books.
- AND MUCH MORE!

Visit **bookfinity.com** and take the fun Reader Type quiz to get started.

Enjoy our classic and modern companion pairings!

Classic & Modern